THE SAMURAI SPIRIT . . .

The Powerful Force Japan Did Not Surrender

By Allan Wagner

Other works by Allan Wagner

Fiction: The Loving Student . . . an American Dream

(available on amazon.com)

Chapter 1

INTRODUCTION

The devastating storms of World War II battered the Pacific and left the warriors of Japan physically exhausted, defeated and in disarray. In defeat the civilian population became disillusioned by the death and destruction the militarists had brought on. Years of propaganda glorifying the imperial empire were shattered and destroyed.

But the end of the war did not bring an end to Japanese culture. A way of life built upon moral training and traditional values would not perish so quickly. Although the humbled nation was forced to rebuild in the postwar era according to the terms of the victors, the ethos of generations past remained in many hearts. The prewar militaristic regimentation, and a glorious tradition of battle, could not be forgotten. At times prewar rituals were remembered in dark, somber shades reflecting bitter memories; on occasion they sparkled in bright tones recalling moments of refined pleasure, as in the tea ceremony or cherry blossom viewing. Some colors in the mosaic of Japan's past culture are still seen, though their original luster no longer shines as brightly as it once did.

One segment of Japanese culture which has survived and evolved since the seventh century is that of the samurai, the sword-fighting hero who stood for right and justice. Japan's neighbors in Asia have criticized it for creating warlike tendencies; the government and militarists have praised it for instilling perseverance and diligence in the nation's subjects. This spirit, a powerful force of inner direction, is innate to the Japanese. The samurai spirit in postwar Japan--whatever it may be--will be analyzed through the lives of Emperor Showa, Japanese Army stragglers, Yukio Mishima, the yakuza, the businessmen, and through other discrepant events, although these are not its only manifestations.

The late Professor Alvin Coox of San Diego State University, a noted historian and author of eight books on Japan's military past, scoffed at the idea of a postwar samurai spirit. "They don't even know what it means any more," he said.[1] Professor Coox based his opinion on the current state of the Japanese Self-Defense Forces (JSDF) and on his personal view of the generations born since1945 into a world of booming trade, economic affluence, and growing luxury-oriented consumerism.

Such criticism may not be entirely fair. There are limitations placed on the JSDF by article IX of the postwar "peace" constitution, which forbids Japan's use of force to settle international disputes. Further interpretation by the Government led to a resolution that Japanese forces would not be used for offensive purposes. Under the PKO (Peace Keeping Operations) law troops can be sent overseas only for peacekeeping missions and must be withdrawn if there are active hostilities. The JSDF also eliminated such strong disciplinary aspects of prewar military training as striking and beating recruits to create an organization different from the Imperial Japanese Army. More emphasis is given to using troops for relief from earthquakes, terrorist attacks and other national disasters. Nonetheless, today's army is equipped with modern field weapons, advanced jet aircraft, close to 300 ships, and operates under a military budget that for many years was the fourth largest in the world. (Note--Surpassed by China in 2009.) Yet within the restrictions placed on it, the JSDF still strives to recall the spirit of the past and inspire today's military with a <u>bushido</u> willingness to defend their country.

True, the hordes of fashionably clothed Ginza shoppers, sing-along bar drinkers, golfers, baseball fans, or souvenir- hungry tourists traveling abroad do not give the impression of a Japan that follows the samurai code. The only samurai-like tendencies that Westerners may see in the Japanese are those used to develop trade policies designed to protect against foreign inroads while promoting the motherland's interests overseas.

However, there are indeed many Japanese who adhere to the traditional values cherished by their ancestors.   Former Ambassador to Japan the late Dr. Edwin O. Reischauer portrayed the contemporary Japanese personality as containing a strong spirit of loyalty, duty, self-discipline, and self-denial,[2] all traits a samurai would prize highly.

Professor Coox's criticism brings out the widely held view that the samurai spirit exemplifies a militaristic, warlike attitude.   In the past the code of bushido meant exactly that: the way of the warrior.   But as recently as the Tokugawa era (1610-1867) the appeal of bushido became widespread and evolved as the ethic of society. In his authoritative history of Japan, Sansom states that the code was by no means the monopoly of the samurai; it set high ideals for all classes.[3]

With the advent of the Meiji Restoration, the samurai fell victim to the democratic process, losing status and becoming no more than an equal among the citizenry, during the de- feudalization of Japan. The new Japanese government introduced laws that did away with the warrior class and banned the carrying of swords, the symbol of the samurai, in public. As a legally recognized class, the samurai ceased to exist although their influence has continued on for another century.

The role of the samurai may have dimmed but their spirit remained untarnished. Starting with the emperor, the leader of the nation, the ethos carried on. During the postwar period the symbolism of the emperor remained largely intact. Emperor Showa retained his symbolic position, if not his theoretically absolute political power. The ethics and morality that he stood for in prewar years were still there for his subjects to emulate. His postwar actions were in large part traceable to the samurai code covering the responsibilities of one's lord.

The exploits of diehard soldiers such as Lieutenant Hiroo Onoda give a different perspective of the code, a view presented by the warrior in the field. The lonely heroism of Onoda, who had been trained to avoid capture and to operate undercover as a guerilla, stirred the admiration of the public in Japan. Onoda carried on for thirty years after the war had officially ended. He became one of the few heroes of the war for the nation's youth, which belatedly learned of his exploits. The adventures of army stragglers, whose actions reflected values central to the samurai code, were relived and applauded in the minds of millions of Japanese who took pride in the achievements of Onoda and others.

Author Yukio Mishima was too young and too sickly to adhere actively to the code during the war. His studies of <u>Hagakure</u>, Japanese history, and the postwar accounts of the Pacific War inspired his transformation into a spiritual, if not a de facto samurai. The samurai ethic motivated him during his life, and he chose to die in samurai style in 1970.

The underworld yakuza organizations claim that they, too, are of samurai descent. These criminal groups have adopted the code of behavior with a particular emphasis on loyalty. Although they represent a small segment of the population, their existence is widely acknowledged.

The appetite of the public for stirring tales of samurai derring-do created a new genre in the motion picture industry: the samurai film and its swashbuckling swordsmen. Popular television adopted the genre too. Movie and television screenplays responded to the postwar search for a national identity, and developed new heroes with characteristics akin to those of the ancient samurai.

The samurai code that the business world followed made good business a benefit for the country. Both the new entrepreneurs and the prewar company executives worked hard in the postwar period to revive Japan. Their efforts were along the same trail blazed almost a century before by the Meiji era samurai. Senior businessmen such as Matsutaro Shoriki represented a renewal of the establishment, while fledgling upstarts such as Giichi Sugimoto created a fresh start under a new democracy. Both were trained in the code of bushido.

Other widely varied events also displayed samurai charisma. Sports figures, terrorists, and bit players in the drama of life all became entwined in the modern samurai culture.

After analyzing each of these aspects of the samurai spirit in postwar Japan, the concluding chapter will touch upon the implications for those who deal with Japan and the Japanese. The existence of a samurai spirit hovering over Japan, a hologram clothed in tradition, encompasses the energy and imagination of much of the nation. The players portray samurai roles--in a sense becoming cultural icons--in the context of modern Japan. They no longer carry swords, but their actions identify them as kindred members of a once-fabled clan.

Notes – Chapter 1

1. Professor Alvin Coox, interview by author, San Diego State University, Fall, 1990.

2. Edwin O. Reischauer, _The Japanese Today_ (Cambridge: Harvard University Press, 1988), 59.

3. Sir George Bailey Sansom, _A History of Japan, 1615-1867_ (Stanford University Press, 1963).

Chapter 2

THE SAMURAI CODE

The samurai are gone.   Their swords are sheathed, sought after only as antique treasures. The spilled blood of samurai campaigns has drained from the battlefields, leaving only memorial tablets and scrolled records of their storied past.   In succumbing, the swashbuckling warriors of yesteryear have bequeathed their descendants with the samurai <u>konjo</u> (spirit). The fearless swordsmen left behind the code that governed their lives and commanded their deaths.   It is a legacy that reverberates to present day Japan.

The warrior class, which comprised about 6 percent of the population,[1]   including soldiers, clerks, and feudal hierarchy, was abolished following the Meiji Restoration of 1868.   The modernization of Japan meant that it was no longer acceptable to stride about with swords at one's waist, ready to cut and slash at your lord's beckoning. The glory days of the samurai, fading slowly during the two hundred and fifty year Tokugawa reign, were officially extinguished by government decree. Long feared, but admired by the farmers and tradespeople, samurai were reduced in rank to become part of the new classless society. The value of being a samurai no longer lay in their force of arms, but in their position as generally literate, aristocratic members of society, and in the samurai heritage, which emanated from the code of bushido. In defining the code, as well as the moral principles involved, it is also necessary to discuss such related factors as Zen and the Japanese concepts of on, giri, and shame.

What is often referred to as the unwritten code of the samurai really has numerous written sources to authenticate it.   Primary among those is Hagakure, the reminiscences of Tsunetomo Yamamoto, a retainer of the Nabeshima clan.   When his lord died in 1700, Yamamoto, who had served him for 42 years, longed to join his lord in death (junshi) by committing disembowelment (seppuku).   However, he was not allowed to do so, because of the reforms introduced during the Tokugawa period.   In an attempt to gain central governmental control of the samurai, retainers were forbidden from practicing junshi upon their lord's death. Instead, Yamamoto retired to a life as a temple priest and, over a period of years, told his story to a young samurai, Tashiro Tsuramoto, who recorded the events and his elder's teachings. Tsuramoto gave the resulting work the title Hagakure (Collection of Leaves).

Hagakure provided a standard for ideal samurai behavior. The teachings were used by the Nabeshima clan to train their retainers, serving as a primer to teach, admonish, and advise. Yamamoto wanted future generations to know the proper manner in which to serve. He passed on the thoughts that he felt were important. "Every morning," he said, "one should first do reverence to his master and parents and then to patron deities and guardian Buddhas." The mental aspects of complete service, body and mind, were emphasized. "For a warrior there is nothing other than thinking of his master."[2]

Yamamoto quoted Hyobu Ooki: "If one's sword is broken, he will strike with his hands. If his hands are cut off, he will press the enemy down with his shoulders. If his shoulders are cut away, he will bite through ten or fifteen enemy necks with his teeth. Courage is such a thing." [3]   Years later, in World War II, General Akira Mutaguchi launched an offensive against the British at Imphal by encouraging his troops with those very words. Mutaguchi embellished them by adding, "if there is breath left in your body, fight with your spirit. Lack of weapons is no excuse for defeat . . . [4]   On that occasion the spirit responded inadequately, however.   The Japanese were defeated.

Loyalty, bravery, death, revenge, shame, harakiri, personal grooming, and even the proper way to bring up a samurai child are all covered in <u>Hagakure</u>.   The only thing lacking is a detailed description of the skirmishes Yamamoto participated in himself.   The work so clearly delineates the ethic of the samurai that many of Yamamoto's sayings appear elsewhere in later sources.

<u>Hagakure</u> ends with four vows:

> Never to be outdone in the Way of
> the Samurai.
> To be of good use to the Master.
> To be filial to one's parents.
> To manifest great compassion, and to act for
> the sake of Man.[5]

Fulfillment of the first vow meant a spartan life of dedication, training, and privation, with eventual death in service a near certainty. A deep resolve to die in a clean, appropriate manner was considered proper. According to Yamamoto, the way of the samurai requires practicing mentally every day, many times over, the experience of death.[6] On a daily basis one should meditate being torn asunder by swords and spears, ripped apart by arrows, shot by rifles, carried away by ocean waves, shaken to death by a giant earthquake, falling from cliffs, dying of disease, or following one's master in death by committing <u>seppuku</u>. Every day one should think of himself as dead.[7]

In chronicles dating from the eleventh century, Paul Varley finds that the true warrior thought of his life as having "no more value than a feather."[8] Long odds with only the barest chance of survival meant nothing because the samurai was prepared to end his life fighting. As a point of honor, he eagerly sought to do combat with the fiercest of enemies.

The samurai code was consistent with the teachings of Zen Buddhism, which reached Japan in the seventh century. Zen rejected rational planning in favor of action that was emotive and intuitive, yet disciplined and controlled. The ultimate sacrifice would be made as an automatic reaction without regard for the consequences.[9]

The samurai rightfully expected to be rewarded for honors won on the battlefield. His reward would not only be personal spiritual fulfillment but also knowing that although he may die, if he served his master well, his wife and children would be cared for as "children of the household." [10] There are also tales of samurai who were rewarded immediately with pieces of gold and silver upon presenting the heads of enemies slain in battle.[11]

A samurai who expected death would be ready for it if he failed in his mission. Without the least hesitation he could cut open his stomach to die, rather than live on in shame. This method of forfeiting one's life, which was considered the most painful, became the samurai's special way of dying with honor. It would smear his name and that of his family, his ancestors, and his descendants with disgrace if he showed any regret at giving up his life . [12]

Seppuku could be committed as an "admonitory disembowelment." [13] If the samurai's advice to his lord were ignored, or to call attention to what he thought was an error in his lord's behavior, the samurai could display his magokoro (sincerity) by committing seppuku. There was no other way to express a deeply held, but contrary, conviction. Loyalty prevented the samurai from criticizing his lord.

To be of good use to the master meant loyalty to an intense degree. "If a warrior makes loyalty and filial piety one load, and courage and compassion another, and carries these 24 hours a day until his shoulders wear out, he will be a samurai."[14]

Varley refers to unswerving devotion as the most redeeming feature of the medieval samurai.[15] Such loyalty became the locus of involved plots and counter plots, spying, and assassinations. Loyalty (giri) to another, higher cause could lead to a betrayal or to a sacrifice. Because of the high moral value placed on loyalty, any violation of it was a shocking event. But lies could be looked upon as part of a strategic plan, according to Mitsuhide Akechi, who betrayed Nobunaga Oda in 1582. Akechi's infamy was revenged only days later when he too was slain, assuring his place in history as "the Thirteen Day Shogun."[16]

In the Japanese interpretation of Confucianism, loyalty to one's lord overcame any other allegiance. From Confucius's words, "act with loyalty in the service of one's lord," total devotion and service to the point of self sacrifice became the samurai creed.

The Chinese took loyalty to mean serving their lord while being true to one's own conscience.[17] The Confucian virtue of filial piety was also interpreted differently. Whereas the Chinese honored family and ancestors, the samurai achieved filial piety by loyally serving his lord. A "suprafamily" group under the lord took precedence, becoming more fundamental than the family itself.[18]

Shoin Yoshida (1830-59), the samurai-philosopher in the late Tokugawa period, wrote "that which has the greatest import for a man is kun-shin no gi (duty of lord and subject)."[19] The seven principles he evolved for the samurai made loyalty part of the first three, with obligations to Amaterasu, the Emperor, and one's lord listed before those owed to one's parents.[20] If a samurai did not show his attachment to the clan, his conduct then evidenced a lack of loyalty, according to Yukichi Fukuzawa.[21] Fukuzawa's autobiography provides first person insights into samurai values. Born in 1835 to a low ranking samurai family, Fukuzawa broke with his samurai roots and left Japan to become exposed to the West. He learned Dutch and English, travelled to Europe and the United States, and studied abroad.   Upon returning to Japan, he became the founder of Keio University. During the Tokugawa period, of which he writes, retainers were expected to die with the Shogun. "That was the way of the faithful warrior."[22]

The famous "Tale of the Forty-Seven Ronin" (Chushingura) illustrates well the loyalty of retainers to their lord. As a play, this story of forty-seven samurai who follow their lord to death by committing seppuku still retains its popularity. Performances are held regularly during each New Year's holiday festivities.

Samurai commitment and loyalty to a cause was demonstrated vividly in October 1876. Some one hundred fifty samurai who felt degraded by the government's commutation of pensions, the ban on wearing swords, and the adoption of foreign clothes and hair style, which did away with the samurai's top knot, made a night attack on a government army garrison at Kumamoto. They killed and wounded three hundred imperial troops. But the samurai were disappointed that their action did not lead to a general uprising to do away with foreign influences. As a show of their sincerity, eighty-four of them committed seppuku.[23]

The moral training of samurai during the Tokugawa period was in accordance with the Japanese interpretation of Confucianism. This philosophy emphasized the virtues of loyalty, righteousness, and propriety for the ruling warrior class, but considered them inapplicable for the lower-ranked farmers, artisans, and tradespeople.[24]   Former samurai used their moral training, reading and writing skills, and social position to become the core of the government bureaucracy in the succeeding Meiji era.

The Meiji Restoration had an interesting effect upon the samurai code as well as upon the samurai. It resulted in what Kazuko Tsurumi refers to as "the samuraization" of non-samurai classes.[25] The common people (heimin) were conscripted into the imperial army and became warriors, although officially there was no longer a warrior class. These new soldiers, under the tutelage of samurai officers and European military instructors, adopted the samurai ethic of loyalty and courage in battle.   Military service was considered crucial to the building of the new government in Japan, for it embodied selfless devotion, even to the point of death. The life of the warrior thus continued to be viewed as having great merit and symbolic importance, while the way of the samurai became open to all in the new class-less society.[26]

Although the Satsuma samurai, led by Takamori Saigo, were defeated in 1877 by the imperial government's conscript army, the Satsuma Rebellion did much to enhance the stalwart image of the samurai warriors.   Saigo's exploits and strategems in combat earned for him the ranking as Japan's greatest samurai. He died In the last battle of the rebellion. Even in defeat Saigo's forces, which were far outnumbered and outgunned, received recognition for their bravery. His valiant stand to retain the rights and position of the samurai, and the ultimate esteem which Saigo gained, were foretold in his own words:

>   "A man of true sincerity will be an example to
> the world even after his death.   When an insincere
> man is spoken well of,   he has, so to speak, got a
> windfall; but a man of deep sincerity will, even if he
> is unknown in his lifetime, have a lasting reward:
> the esteem of posterity."[27]

The imperial forces, which had been trained by European officers, were eager to prove their discipline and efficiency. They were motivated to meet the same valiant standards as their opponents. In addition to the heimin (common people) conscripts, the imperial army in the early years of the Meiji era was also comprised of many former samurai.[28]

The Imperial Rescript on Education, issued October 30, 1890, gave governmental endorsement to concepts inherent in the samurai code.[29] Loyalty and filial piety as expounded in the rescript became part of the country's national education, included in the curriculum for morals classes in the schools. Loyalty officially started with fealty to the Emperor as the symbol of the national polity. Dying for one's lord was transferred to a higher plane: the goal of dying an honorable death for the Emperor.[30] The samurai ethic of feudal days was thus carried forward into the Meiji era and beyond.

Hagakure Nyumon (The Way of the Samurai) by Yukio Mishima is an introduction to Hagakure, which explains much of the original with comments by Mishima. Written in the post-World War II period, it cited examples of samurai-like behavior, such as the kamikaze pilots of the Pacific War. Mishima lamented the tarnished image of the kamikaze pilots, but offered them as the best example of samurai. "The spirit of those young men who for the sake of their country hurled themselves to certain death is closest in the long history of Japan to the clear ideal of action and death offered in Hagakure," he stated.[31]

Mishima interpreted and redefined the samurai code, but could add nothing to it, as the age of the samurai had long since passed. But he did not consider it passé. With his own nationalistic bent, Mishima sought to use the code to influence Japanese public opinion. "I see it as showing human beings in certain fixed conditions, the guiding principles . . . universal teachings, practical knowledge based on practical experience, " he wrote. [32]

Ruth Benedict in her classic study The Chrysanthemum and the Sword defined Japanese morality as a morality of shame, one in which the samurai would value external appearances.[33] Mishima agreed with Benedict, stating that morality which concentrates on external reflection is the essential characteristic described in Hagakure.[34]

Mishima criticized the post-World War II Japanese, regretting the passing of the samurai and the demise of the samurai spirit. "Strict samurai instruction from father to son is completely neglected . . . the father is reduced to a machine that brings home a paycheck," he said.[35]

A more conventional description of the way of the samurai appears in Inazo Nitobe's Bushido, The Soul of

Japan, originally published in 1905. Nitobe, one of Japan's first post-restoration scholars, wrote in English with a view to explaining his country's traditions to the Western world.

Nitobe described valor, loyalty, honor, the ceremonial process of seppuku, and other rituals of the samurai and was lavish in his praise of the bushido code of ethics. "Bushido was and still is the animating spirit, the motor force of our country," he wrote.[36] Nitobe thought the entire nation to be imbued with this spirit. "Scratch a Japanese of the most advanced ideas, and he will show a Samurai," Nitobe said.[37] As a code of ethics, bushido may disappear, but according to Nitobe "its power will not perish from the earth; its schools of martial prowess or civic honor may be demolished, but its light and glory will long survive their ruins."[38]

The history of Japan leading to World War II, the destruction of the country, and its rebirth in the postwar period appear to reflect Nitobe's prediction. The power of the samurai code motivated many Japanese during the war and continued to do so in the postwar period.

Writing at about the same time as Nitobe, Lafcadio Hearn, who knew Japan as well as any Westerner of his day, expressed similar thoughts about what he termed "the religion of loyalty," an integral part of the samurai code although it is not generally referred to as a religion. In <u>Japan, An Attempt at Interpretation</u>, Hearn considered the combination of loyalty and filial piety as a factor of "incalculable worth" following the Meiji Restoration. "What wonders it has wrought, within the space of thirty years," he wrote.[39]

The feudal samurai code did not fade away with the Meiji Restoration, but became more widespread through the equalization of the social classes and its incorporation into the national educational system. Allegiance to the samurai's lord was transferred to the Emperor with the resurgence of the imperial position during the Meiji period. The obligations owed to the Emperor were reiterated until they virtually became a way of life for his subjects. The willingness to die prescribed to by the samurai class continued on as a main pillar of the military code of the new imperial army. Japanese warriors who engaged in battle in the modern era retained the image of their ancestors by fighting to the death, rather than facing the humiliation of surrender.

Notes - Chapter 2

1. Reischauer, 72.

2. Tsunetomo Yamamoto, Hagakure, trans. William Scott Wilson (Tokyo: Kodansha International Ltd., 1979), 23.

3. Ibid., 107. Evidently Ooki was a contemporary figure. He is not listed in Japan Biographical Encyclopedia & Who's Who, nor is he cited in the indexes of Battles of the Samurai or The Samurai, A Military History.

4. Arthur Swinson, Four Samurai (London: Hutchinson & Co., 1968), 141.

5. Yamamoto, 169.

6 . Ibid., 73.

7. Ibid., 164.

8. Paul H. Varley with Ivan and Nobuko Morris. Samurai (New York: Delacorte Press, 1970), 22.

9. Ibid., 45.

10. Ibid., 23.

11. S.R. Turnbull, The Samurai, A Military History (New York: Macmillan Publishing Co., 1977), 191.

12. Ibid., 72.

13. Varley, 33.

14. Yamamoto, 95.

15. Varley, 67.

16. Turnbull, 162-165.

17. Michio Morishima, Why Has Japan 'Succeeded'?

(Cambridge: Cambridge University Press, 1982), 7. In China benevolence was the central virtue of Confucianism, while in Japan no special importance was given to it.

18. Reischauer, 58.

19. David Magarey Earl, Emperor and Nation in Japan (Seattle: University of Washington Press, 1964), translation by Earl from Yoshida Shoin Zenshu, 131.

20. Ibid., 182.

21. Yukichi Fukuzawa, The Autobiograhpy of Fukuzawa Yukichi, trans. Eiichi Kiyooka (New York: Columbia University Press, 1966), 183.

22. Ibid., 195.

23. Augustus H. Mounsey, The Satsuma Rebellion (London: John Murray, 1879; reprinted by University Publications of America, Washington, D.C., 1979), 92.
24. Morishima, 49.

25. Kazuko Tsurumi, Social Change and the Individual (Princeton: Princeton University Press, 1970), 86. Robert N. Bellah, Tokugawa Religion (New York: The Free Press, 1957) says that the cornmon people were "bushido-ized."

26. Robert N. Bellah, Tokugawa Religion (New York: The Free Press, 1957), 97. Bellah's work is based on the writings of such leading historical figures as Soko Yamaga (Bukyo Shogaku), Shoin Yoshida, and Shingen Takeda, as well as the Nabeshima clan which Yamamoto depicted in Hagakure. Bellah terms bushido a religion of loyalty, but as a caveat notes the influences of Confucianism, militarism, and a preoccupation with death (91). Zen is encouraged to lead the samurai in his mental preparation toward the acceptance of death. "The practice of the Zen has no secret, except standing on the verge of life and death," wrote Shingen Takeda, a sixteenth century warlord.

27. Ivan Morris, The Nobility of Failure (New York: Holt, Rinehart and Winston), 243, quoting Moriaki Sakamoto Nanshu-O's (Saigo Takamori's) Posthumous Words, unpublished manuscript, 32.

28. Mounsey, 118.

29. U.S. Department of the Army,   SCAP, Political Reorientation of Japan, Sept. 1945-Sept. 1948 (Washington, D.C.: Government Printing Office, 1949), trans. Foreign Affairs Association of Japan, compo The Japan Yearbook, 1935 (Tokyo: Kenkyusha Press, 1935)

781-782.

30.Bellah, 82.
31. Yukio Mishima, The Way of the Samurai, trans.
Kathryn Sparling (New York: Putnam Publishing Group,
1983), 101.
32. Ibid., 40.
33. Ruth Benedict, The Chrysanthemum and the Sword
(Boston: Houghton Mifflin Co., 1946), 222-224.

34. Mishima, 59.
35. Mishima, 64.

36. Inazo Nitobe, Bushido, The Soul of Japan (New
York: G.P. Putnam's Sons, 1905), 171.
37. Ibid., 188.
38. Ibid., 192.

39. Lafcadio Hearn, Japan, An Attempt at Interpretation
(New York: Grosset & Dunlap, 1904), 329.

Chapter 3

THE SHOWA EMPEROR

As the imperial monarch of Japan, the actions and statements of Hirohito, the Showa Emperor, claimed the attention of the Japanese nation.   The media dutifully kept Hirohito's presence in front of the people by reporting his daily activities, printing and broadcasting his public statements, and following the upbringing of the imperial family, and in particular Crown Prince Akihito, in the postwar era.   In addition to his being the titular head of the country, there   were several instances where the Emperor's actions in the public spotlight provided examples of the samurai code, his conduct becoming a model for the nation to follow.

The Emperor's position changed drastically in the postwar period. He no longer paraded about on his stallion, White Snow, as the stalwart leader of the Imperial Japanese Army.   Instead, he withdrew to become a benevolent figurehead who projected a humble aura of peace, harmony, and goodwill toward humankind.   Symbolically quiet work as a marine biologist became his primary public guise, replacing the military trappings once associated with his office.

In 1987 when the slowly failing health of Emperor Hirohito became a matter of national concern, that the Emperor was dying was a fact no one could deny, but few would discuss. In addition to the breach of etiquette involved in discussing an impending death, the national reverence for the Emperor did not allow for such discussion. In the nouveau riche modernity of the country, there remained a sacred institution that could not be defiled. The Emperor resided in the hearts of the majority of the people as the living symbol of the nation.

After Hirohito's death on January 7, 1989, there was no taboo on discussion about the Emperor, but when Nagasaki's mayor, Hitoshi Motoshima, openly stated that the Emperor bore some moral responsibility for the war, it became a cause celebre and led to an attempted assassination of the mayor. Leftists had long argued precisely the same point that Motoshima made, but for a public official supported by the conservative Liberal Democratic Party (LDP) to do so was unconscionable. The ultranationalist fringe angered by Motoshima's statements felt duty-bound to protect the good name of the Emperor. Moreover, the mayor lost the political backing of the LDP, which sought to disassociate itself

from such statements.[1]   In the Spring 1991 election
when Motoshima sought a fourth term as mayor the LDP
refused to back him, although he was considered an
overwhelming favorite. The popular mayor merely
switched parties, running and winning under the banner
of the Social Democratic Party.[2]

The assassination attempt was not an isolated
incident.   Others who criticized the Emperor's role,
among them writers and educators, were also threatened
by ultranationalists. In January 1989,
novelist-playwright Hisashi Inoue took part in a
newspaper- sponsored roundtable discussion of the
Emperor's role in the war and became the victim of a
series of telephone threats: "You're dead meat, Inoue. I
don't know when, but I'll get you."   Hate mail which
included dead cockroaches and a razor blade, to suggest
suicide, followed.[3]

While fringe groups can be dismissed as just
that--minor factions on the outskirts of mainstream
thought--during the Emperor's lengthy illness, the depth
of reverential feeling among the bulk of the populace
became evident.   The benign, bespectacled figure
Tsurumi referred to as "the benevolent father of the
whole nation" lay dying.[4]   Still etched deeply in many

minds remained the ancient concept of <u>kokutai</u> wherein the Emperor's will was the will of the gods and the people's will was the Emperor's will, and to be "sincere" meant to have a pure heart united with the Emperor and the gods.[5]   Officially, Shinto was no longer the state religion of Japan, but who could tell?   The separation of church and state in the postwar constitution did little to remove Shintoism from the scene.   Democratization went no further than institutional and legal reform; it did not change the social structure, the way of life, or "the mental constitution of the people."[6]   When government funding was no longer available to maintain the thousands of Shinto shrines throughout the country, voluntary groups, many of whose members were rightwingers and former military officers, formed service groups to clean and maintain the shrines.[7]   They willingly responded to the calling of their heritage, to Shinto, and to the leadership of the Emperor.

Indigenous to Japan, Shinto was developed from an early animistic religion, which predated the entry of Buddhism.   In ancient times the religion, which bears similarities to Chinese Taoism, was primarily followed by the imperial family, but through the holy blessings of harvests, festivals, marriages, and ground breakings it spread to the general population.   By the eleventh century Shinto earned recognition as the national religion. Shintoism promoted the Japanese spirit through self- sacrifice for the benefit of the Emperor and the country.[8]

In prewar Japan it would have been unthinkable to criticize the Emperor, while in the postwar era, although the concept of lese majeste was no longer valid, there was little desire to do so. But for those who would, the thinly veiled threat of retaliation from the far right extremists hovered in the background.   The ultranationalist logic remained enmeshed in the prewar interpretation of Emperor worship and a belief that a righteous cause was the proper one. They regarded the Emperor as one who could do no wrong, "the culmination of the True, the Good, and the Beautiful."[9] The period of national concern as the Emperor's health declined saw a resurgence of nationalism in Japan.

The ultranationalists were protecting values that the Emperor himself had officially abandoned in 1945.   At that moment in history, with defeat imminent, the Emperor addressed his "good and loyal subjects" and told them he had ordered the government to accept the Potsdam Declaration, bringing to an end Japan's hopes for a Greater East Asia Co-Prosperity Sphere.   "We have resolved to pave the way for a grand peace for all the generations to come by enduring the unendurable and suffering what is unsufferable," he said .[10]

Preparing oneself to endure the bitter taste of defeat was part of the discipline of resignation, as explained in Hagakure. The state of resignation could be attained by daily embracing the proverb, "True patience lies in bearing what is unbearable."[11]

Less than two weeks after Japan's formal surrender aboard the U.S.S. Missouri in Tokyo Bay on September 15, 1945, the Emperor paid a call on the Supreme Commander for the Allied Powers (SCAP) General Douglas MacArthur.   For the first time in Japanese history the Emperor called upon a foreign dignitary. The two met with only the Emperor's interpreter present.   In his memoirs, MacArthur described the meeting: "We sat down before an open fire at one end of the long reception hall.   I offered him an American cigarette, which he took with thanks. I noticed how his hands shook as I lighted it for him.   I tried to make it as easy for him as I could, but I knew how deep and dreadful must be his agony of humiliation. I had an uneasy feeling he might plead his own cause against indictment as a war criminal." [12]

The Emperor had no such intention. Instead, the monarch's samurai heritage rose to the occasion. "I come to you, General MacArthur," he said, "to offer myself to the judgment of the powers you represent as the one to bear sole responsibility for every political and military decision made and action taken by my people in the conduct of war." [13]   In the Japanese accounts of the historic meeting, given four days later at a press conference by a spokesman of the Ministry of Horne Affairs, the Emperor was quoted as being impressed with MacArthur and well satisfied with the progress of the occupation, and MacArthur responded that "the smooth occupation was really due to the Emperor's leadership."   The emperor's offer to bear responsibility was not mentioned.[14]   The intentions of the Allied powers, of which MacArthur was aware but the Emperor was not, did not include indictment of the Emperor.

The Emperor made a similar statement during the last conference with his wartime cabinet before ending hostilities. Under normal circumstances the Emperor endorsed government decisions presented to him. In this instance the cabinet could not agree on ending the war--the military being adamantly opposed to the terms of the Potsdam Declaration. It marked one of the few times in history that the Japanese monarch decided what the government would do. The Emperor told his ministers, who were concerned about the survival of the imperial system, to accept the Potsdam Declaration and save the nation. "I am not concerned with what may happen to me. I want to preserve the lives of the people," he said. [15]

The widely printed picture of MacArthur and the Emperor taken on that first visit of September 27, 1945, shows the Emperor standing formally in a cutaway coat and striped trousers, with the general, sans jacket, looking casual in summer khaki with an open collar. While MacArthur may have felt compassion for his former enemy, the general's manner of dress did not appear proper for meeting a head of state. The photo, carried on the front pages of the nation's newspapers, was interpreted by many as further evidence of Japan's humiliation. "The shock was like a hammer blow. . . . It conveyed better than a thousand words the reality of Japan's defeat and the new, subordinate position of the Emperor."[16] Biographer Clayton James notes however that MacArthur regularly avoided wearing a dress uniform, "no matter how distinguished the visitor," preferring khaki with an open-necked shirt.[17]

The Emperor had surrendered his empire; he had also offered his life. He had shown the samurai military virtues of honor, self discipline, and a willingness to die. His plight as he stood before his enemy was well documented. Some twenty years later, the Emperor recalled his impressions of MacArthur as a just man, one of faith, who had great knowledge of East Asia. The Emperor termed his first meeting with MacArthur as his most unforgettable event in the postwar period.[18]

The character of the Emperor allowed him to place his trust in MacArthur. Kantaro Suzuki, prime minister at the end of the war, said the Emperor commanded him to confide in the enemy and place everything at the conqueror's disposal. Suzuki said the Emperor felt the same way he did, "that was to trust the enemy commander." He added, "The 'Bushido' is not a Japanese monopoly. It is a universal code. To protect your adversary who has surrendered as one enlisted on your side is the way of the warrior . . . I myself as a soldier had a firm trust in this soldierly spirit."[19]

(Although the Emperor and Suzuki may have felt that way, the war record of the Japanese did not indicate a policy of protection for an adversary who has surrendered – quite the contrary.)

On January I, 1946, in his New Year's message to the people, the Emperor denied his divinity. "The ties between us and our people have always stood upon mutual trust and affection. They do not depend on the false conception that the Emperor is divine and that the Japanese people are superior to other races," his imperial rescript proclaimed. Citing the Charter Oath of his grandfather, Emperor Meiji, he emphasized that "all measures of government [shall be] decided in accordance with public opinion."[20]   The rescript attempted to bridge the gap between the initial attempt at democracy under Emperor Meiji and a new democratic beginning for Japan. Marius Jansen makes the point that Emperor Meiji and Emperor Showa both needed a break with the immediate past, and both used imperial rescripts to present the new direction the nation would take.[21] Emperor Showa had grown up admittedly enamored of his grandfather, stating later that he always kept Emperor Meiji's deeds in mind.[22]

With his actions to end the war, to offer himself to the enemy, and to declare an end to the concept of his divinity, the Emperor, in the best of samurai traditions, bore full responsibility for the people he perceived to be under his care. He was repaying the <u>chu</u>, the loyalty of the common man to the Emperor, which he had received.

From ancient times neither <u>giri</u> nor loyalty was considered one-sided. A lord who received loyalty repaid it in the care he took and the stipends he provided for his samurai. The samurai and their families could expect to be looked after according to their position and the obligations they were under.[23] The lord also faced a debt of loyalty to his retainers, one that the Showa Emperor showed a willingness to acknowledge toward the people of Japan. The Emperor felt bound by the social obligations which commanded his people's allegiance. The price he would repay would be the greater because his position as the ultimate authority figure was so exalted.

But the new rulers of Japan had other plans for the Emperor. MacArthur recognized the importance of the Emperor's sanctity and the difference having him in place would make during the occupation. MacArthur warned the United States government of the potentially dire consequences of attempting to govern Japan without the Emperor: he estimated the occupation force would require at least one million troops to control what might then be an unruly populace. "His [the Emperor's] indictment will unquestionably cause a tremendous convulsion among the Japanese people, the repercussions of which cannot be overestimated. He is the symbol which unites all the Japanese. Destroy him and the nation will disintegrate," MacArthur said.[25]

Washington responded favorably to MacArthur's opinion. The Emperor would not be tried for war crimes, instead he would become a figurehead in the new Japanese government. A letter from the State-War-Navy Coordinating Committee (SWNCC), the group overseeing prosecution of the war, directed MacArthur "to assist secretly in popularizing and humanizing the Emperor" unbeknownst to the Japanese people. MacArthur and his staff were to create a new interpretation of the imperial system.[26]

MacArthur's post-surrender orders did not say the imperial system should be abolished. The Emperor was to be used as long as he furthered Allied goals for the occupation.[27] By the terms of the Potsdam Declaration, the form of Japan's government would be determined by the free will of the Japanese people; they would decide the fate of the Emperor.

The British government also anticipated that the Emperor would remain in place. In December 1945 when a Member of Parliament asked about the wartime culpability of the Emperor, the government stated that it did not propose to indict the Emperor. He was too important in the postwar control of Japan. "Without the Emperor there is no chance of anything but chaos and the ultimate revival of the ideology of aggression," the government said. The response was given in written form to avoid the publicity attendant upon such a discussion in Parliament.[28] But the Allies were not united on this point. In May 1946 Radio Moscow called for the prosecution of the Emperor, and Australia and New Zealand told MacArthur that Hirohito should be first on the list of war criminals.[29]

There is no evidence that MacArthur ever tried to comply with the SWNCC directive by manipulating the Emperor, nor was there a need to. According to MacArthur, Emperor Showa displayed a cooperative attitude and was eager for the rebirth of his country along democratized lines. "I found he had a more thorough grasp of the democratic concept than almost any Japanese with whom I talked. He played a major role in the spiritual regeneration of Japan, and his loyal cooperation and influence had much to do with the success of the occupation."[30]

On December 9, 1945, the Yomiuri Hochi Shimbun
stated that 95 percent of the people supported the
imperial system, the claim being based upon an opinion
poll that the newspaper had sponsored.[31]   Another
survey done by the Yomiuri Shimbun in mid- 1948
showed 90.3 percent of the respondents favoring
continuation of the position of Emperor. [32]

In the months following the war, when the public
learned of the rubble and debris surrounding the imperial
palace, spontaneous "sweeping brigades" formed to
clean the grounds. The practice took hold and has
continued.   For 3 - 4 days each year volunteers come by
bus and train from the hinterlands to pull up weeds and
pick up dead leaves.   More than a million persons have
proudly participated since the war, lending their support
to the Emperor. The Emperor recognized the efforts of
his people by presenting them with tours of the inner
palace and with cigarettes and rice cakes bearing the
imperial crest.   There has never been a shortage of
applicants for this homage to the Emperor.[33]

The government presented a draft of the new
constitution to the public on May 6, 1946. According to
Shinichi Fujii, it "may be said to have been 'created' in
conformity with strong advice liberally accorded by

[SCAP]." [34]

The Emperor read the new constitution and approved it at once, even though it would reduce the power of the throne and assign to the government the biggest part of the Emperor's personal estate. The Diet adopted the new constitution late in 1946 and it went into effect in May 1947. The document changed the Emperor's status from an absolute monarch into a constitutional one, although still referring to him as "the symbol of the state and unity of the people."[35]

The separation of religion from the state and the antiwar clauses of Article IX of the Constitution were two other well known changes.[36] Reischauer described the new constitution as "compatible with Japanese political experience" and "enthusiastically embraced" by the great majority.[37] While the great majority may be more accepting of it than enthusiastic, the constitution has not been revised since going into effect.

Although SCAP encouraged public debate of the Emperor's role in the war and the continuance of the imperial system, little such discussion took place. Comments critical of the Emperor were limited, possibly because of Japan's only recent history of authoritarian thought control.[38] According to one source, during the

Occupation one of Japan's postwar prime ministers abruptly left a social gathering of foreigners when he found himself in the midst of a discussion of the Emperor.   The next day he called the host Occupation official and apologized for his sudden departure.   "I was greatly embarrassed," he said, "to find myself participating in such a discussion of His Majesty."[39]

The postwar message presented to the Japanese people could only have strengthened their belief in the Emperor: they saw their military dismantled and previous heroes stand trial as war criminals for their deeds, but the Emperor remained in place, recognized as a viable entity by the Occupation.   Even with the military flame strongly stamped out, the Emperor's light continued on as a guiding beacon. The Emperor faced his insufferable burden as a weight carried in zazen (deep meditative state of Zen in which the subject overcomes his present surroundings), and remained true to his principles. Instead of the lofty presence he had been in the past, generally unseen and protected from the public except for special occasions, the Emperor became a role model for peaceful Japanese behavior.

Yet, years later, when he was asked, "Could Your Majesty compare your prewar and postwar roles?" He replied, "I don't think there has been any change, spiritually, in my prewar and postwar roles. I feel I have always acted in strict observance of the constitution."[40]

The Emperor had become the symbolic leader of a democratic nation. His reign was now reduced to that of an appendage to the body politic, its legitimate basis being the cultural heritage he represented as the 125th occupant of the Chrysanthemum Throne. Despite the years of anguish at home and abroad that had been caused by the war, the Emperor and the imperial system he headed remained in place, weakened but surviving. His status as monarch had moved backward in time, closer to what it had been in the pre-Meiji Restoration era. At that time the Emperor offered more of a symbol than outright rule, indeed as emperors had done throughout much of Japan's history.

After the drama and excitement of war, the postwar years became almost routine. In 1946 the Emperor embarked on a series of tours, including visits to Chiba, Aichi, Gifu, and Ibaraki prefectures. The Emperor's travels were referred to as his "humanization" campaign, helping to emphasize the fact that he should no longer be looked upon as a divine personage. He encouraged the people in their rebuilding efforts and everywhere met with throngs of well-wishers. Imperial chamberlain Kanroji Osanaga noted the effects of the Emperor's influence as he traveled around the country. The people greeted him with adulation wherever he went, even to the extent of having his feet inadvertently stepped on by crowds eager to get close to him. Osanaga quotes author Takashi Nagai (The Bells of Nagasaki) who described the Emperor as a "devout pilgrim" on a mission "to pay his respects to the souls of those who died in the war."[41] The Emperor visited another twenty-one prefectures in 1947, everywhere propounding the principles of equality in accordance with the new Japanese Constitution.

The Imperial Household Agency carefully planned the Emperor's schedule. It included all the mandatory appearances for holidays and religious ceremonies, two days or more a week for his studies in marine biology, and sufficient time for his children and grandchildren. The Emperor continued to receive the credentials of foreign ambassadors and to meet ceremonially with dignitaries from other nations.

Both the continuation of the imperial system and a warm, favorable attitude toward the Emperor were reinforced through his many appearances, including such popular events as the marriage of Crown Prince Akihito to a commoner, Michiko Shoda;   the opening ceremonies of the Tokyo Olympic Games; his goodwill tour of Europe in 1971, and his visit to Disneyland in 1975.   During these years the unprecedented growth of Japan's economy added to the generally rosy picture.

By the time the Emperor died on January 7, 1989, Japan had reached a position of global leadership in many fields.   Accordingly, the world responded to his demise with an outpouring of expressions of admiration for the Emperor.   Although the publicity generated by the Emperor's death brought forth some questions about his wartime culpability, such remonstrations were largely submerged by the praise for his position as leader during Japan's rebirth and its ascendance as a world power.   Upon his death more than three million mourners visited palace sites in Japan to offer their condolences [42]

The Emperor's funeral became a solemn undertaking which carefully separated the traditional ceremony appropriate for a head of state from religious Shinto rites. The government made a great effort "to separate the funeral from any of the religious connotations that would reflect the chauvinism of the war years and the really nationalistic forms of Shinto," according to Professor John Dower.[43]   Held on February 24, 1989, the funeral assembled the largest international gathering of its kind with 55 heads of state and 164 countries represented.[44]

Nippon Hoso Kyokai (NHK) broadcast the funeral in its entirety, covering the entire route of the procession. Despite the cold rain that day, crowds lined the streets bowing their heads as the hearse with the chrysanthemum seal slowly went by.   Faces were filled with sorrow and tears. The police band played a dirge, while 20,000 policemen controlled the route.   NHK reviewed the Emperor's life, showing pictures of the empress, his family, and his grandchildren.   The Emperor's last poem was read.   And, as a final humanizing touch, among the personal items buried with the Emperor was his beloved Mickey Mouse watch,[45] a reminder perhaps of unity with the people in the enjoyment of simple pleasures.

The funeral riveted the nation's attention.   Pan shots on NHK showed Tokyo's normally bustling streets void of cars and people.   In Shinjuku, along the route of the funeral procession, the area's thirty-seven theaters and nineteen department stores were all closed.[46]

However, in the spirit of democracy, there were also pockets of apathy and opposition to the Emperor. At Ueno Station, the trains heading north to the ski slopes were packed with young people taking advantage of the holiday, while in Tokyo's Shiba Park, the police watched warily as a small group demonstrated against the imperial system.[47]

In spite of the war questions, and even the opposition that it raised, the occasion of the Emperor's death provided another successful hearing for the principles which he followed during his life. As Emperor he fought his battles in diplomatic fashion, using the pen, the spoken word, and his presence as his weapons. On those occasions when they were needed--to end the war, in meeting with MacArthur, by suffering the unsufferable, or in leading his people during the postwar era--he managed his tools skillfully. He had represented his people well. The heritage of bushido, the powerful innate force, in many ways at the core of his existence, stayed within his being, there for him to draw upon, and he did, as the Lord in a nation of samurai. In defeat the Japanese were able to fall back upon the samurai code to move forward.

Notes - Chapter 3

1.   Hisashi Inoue, "As New Leader, Japan Needs To Confront the Past Honestly," Japan Times, trans. Asia Foundation Translation Service Center, weekly international edition (24 Sept. 1990).

2. "LDP Discards Motoshima for Nagasaki Mayoral Race," Japan Times, weekly international edition (11 March 1991).

3. Ibid., 8.

4. Kazuko Tsurumi, Social Change and the Individual (Princeton: Princeton University Press, 1970), 93.

5. Robert N. Bellah, Tokugawa Religion (New York: The Free Press, 1957), 104.

6. Masao Maruyama, "Nationalism in Japan: Its Theoretical Background and Prospects," Chuo Koron, 1951, trans. David Titus in Thought and Behavior in Modern Japanese Politics, ed. Ivan Morris (London: Oxford University Press, 1963), 151.

7. Ibid., 151.

8. Michio Morishima, Why Has Japan 'Succeeded'? (Cambridge: Cambridge University Press, 1982), 36-40.

9. Ivan Morris, "Theory and Psychology of Ultra-Nationalism", <u>Sekai</u>, May 1946 in <u>Thought and Behavior in Modern Japanese Politics</u>, 9.

10. <u>Imperial Rescript Ending the War</u>, trans. U.S. Department of the Army, Supreme Commander for Allied Powers, "Reports of General MacArthur" (Washington, D.C.: Government Printing Office, 1967) •

11. Hiroshi Minami, <u>Psychology of the Japanese People</u>, trans. Albert R. Ikoma (Tokyo: University of Tokyo Press, 1971), 51.

12. Douglas A. MacArthur, <u>Reminiscences</u> (New York: McGraw- Hill, 1964), 288.

13. Ibid., 288.

14. D. Clayton James, <u>The Years of MacArthur</u>, 3 (Boston: Houghton Mifflin Co., 1985), 322.

15. Kanroji Osanaga, <u>Hirohito: An Intimate Portrait of the Japanese Emperor</u>. (Los Angeles: Gateway Publishers, Inc., 1975), 132.

16. Toshiaki Kawahara, <u>Hirohito and His Times</u> (Tokyo: Kodansha International Ltd., 1990), 145.

17. James, 358. MacArthur was also photographed in similar garb during ceremonies with President Syghman Rhee of South Korea and with American President Harry

Truman.

18. "Emperor Recalls Meeting M'Arthur, " <u>Japan Times</u> (26 Aug. 1965), 4.

19. MacArthur, 279 (quoting translation of <u>Mainichi Shimbun</u> article by Suzuki sent to him by Prime Minister Shigeru Yoshida in August, 1946).

20. <u>Imperial Rescript</u>, Jan. 1, 1946, trans. U.S. Dept. of Army, SCAP, "Political Reorientation of Japan" (Washington, D.C.: Government Printing Office, 1949), Appendix, 470.

21. Marius B. Jansen, "Monarchy and Modernization In Japan," <u>Journal of Asian Studies</u> 36 (1977), 611.

22. Bernard Krisher, "A Talk with the Emperor of Japan," <u>Newsweek</u> (29 Sept. 1975), 56.

23. Minami, 159.

24. Takie Sugiyama Lebra, <u>Japanese Patterns of Behavior</u> (Honolulu: University of Hawaii Press, 1976), 14.

25. Edward Behr, <u>Hirohito: Behind the Myth</u> (London: Hamish Hamilton, 1989) quoting letter from MacArthur to the Joint Chiefs of Staff, dated Jan. 25, 1946; 410.

26. Ibid., quoting July 1946 directive from SWNCC in

Washington, D.C., 426.

27. Kiyoko Takeda, The Dual Image of the Japanese Emperor (London: MacMillan Education Ltd., 1988), 107.

28. Ibid., 26.,

29..Ibid. , 176

30. MacArthur, 288

31.Cited in Takeda, 122.

32.Ibid., 177.
33.Kawahara, 156.
34. Shinichi Fujii, The Constitution of Japan (Tokyo: Kokushikan University, 1965), 282. Justin Williams, Sr., Japan's Political Revolution Under MacArthur (Athens: University of Georgia Press, 1979), 114-117, and Theodore H. McNelly, "'Induced Revolution': The Policy and Process of Constitutional Reform in Occupied Japan," Democratizing Japan, ed. Robert E. Ward and Yoshikazu Sakamoto (Honolulu: University of Hawaii Press, 1987), 82-84, explain SCAP's strong presentation of a model draft which the Japanese rewrote and modified.   Changes in the draft were made after SCAP review and approval.
35. MacArthur, 301.
36. The constitution is reviewed in Japan's Commission

on the Constitution: The Final Report, trans. and ed.
John M. Maki (Seattle: University of Washington Press,
1980).

37. Reischauer, 106.

38. Takeda, 111.

39. Allan R. Brown, "The Figurehead Role of the
Japanese Emperor: Perception and Reality," (Ph.D. diss.,
Stanford University, 1971), 29. Brown did not identify
the source.

40. Quoted in Krisher, 56.

41. Osanaga, 135.

42. Jon Funabiki. "Course of Japan's Future Weighed
by View of Past," San Diego Union (8 Jan. 1989).

43. Quoted in Jon Funabiki, "Two Hirohito Ceremonies
May Show Confusion on Role of Emperor," San Diego
Union (11 Jan. 1989).

44. Kawahara, 4.

45. NHK telecast, trans. by author (24 Feb. 1989).

46. Ibid.

47. Ibid.

Chapter 4

JAPANESE ARMY STRAGGLERS

In postwar Japan, after the initial shock of defeat and a lengthy pause for a dazed public to recover, there was a resurgence of interest in the record of the Japanese military. The history of the nation's war machine could finally be revealed as it really happened, without fear of censorship by the Occupation authorities. Memoirs by war veterans and "final accounts" of battles enjoyed a boom in Japanese newspapers and magazines through the 1950s.[1] Readers included the serious minded, ex-soldiers and their relatives, and a growing segment of impressionable young readers. One magazine specializing in war stories estimated that after each monthly issue it received 1,000 letters from readers, the majority from teenage boys. The exploits of the military were detailed regularly, with special editions and extras. One publisher carne out with a supplement of popular war songs.[2] A new generation of Japanese youth was finding its national identity through glorious accounts of engagements with the enemy.

Among these stories were those of wartime stragglers, men who fought on after Japan's official surrender. These were tales of soldiers who persevered, refusing to surrender. None showed the traits of loyalty and devotion to duty better than Lieutenant Hiroo Onoda.

"What could I do to persuade you to come out of the jungle?"

"I won't give in until I have direct orders," Onoda answered. He gave the young Japanese confronting him in 1974 the name of Major Taniguchi, his immediate superior.[3]

After thirty years of deprivation in the jungles of the Philippines, Onoda was still waiting for orders before he would surrender. He did not believe that World War II had ended, that Japan had been defeated. Onoda was not alone in his belief in the invincibility of Imperial Japan. Not until sixteen years after the war had ended were soldiers Masashi Ito and Bunzo Minagawa found in the jungles of Guam. Later, after twenty-eight years of living alone in an underground cave, also on Guam, Sergeant Shoichi Yokoi was finally captured and returned to Japan.

What was the motivation that kept these men at war? Why did they endure years of an animal-like existence, facing disease, loneliness, and starvation? What is it they believed in so strongly that they would face unbearable conditions, yet still survive? The biographical accounts of these wartime samurai shows much of what influenced them--the indoctrination and training given Japanese soldiers.

The pre-World War II Japanese army adamantly enforced discipline. Soldiers had to follow orders to the letter. To emphasize this one regimental commander who took his troops out for a fifty-mile march ordered that no one touch their water canteen. Twenty men passed out from exhaustion and dehydration. Five died. When the bodies were examined, their water canteens were still full.[4] This unswerving discipline was based on respect for the authority of superiors--even the authority of corporals and sergeants--and for what it represented to the common soldier: an order from the Emperor, recognized as the supreme commander of the armed forces.[5]

Loyalty to the Emperor was inculcated in the Japanese people from birth and was reinforced by both the role of the Emperor in a Confucian society and the country's educational system. The Imperial Rescript on Education, hammered home in the public school system, told the Emperor's subjects to "offer yourself courageously to the State and thus guard and maintain the prosperity of Our Imperial Throne coeval with heaven and earth."

Emperor Meiji's Imperial Rescript to Soldiers and Sailors cited loyalty first among the essential duties of a soldier. As part of the Meiji constitution, the rescript made loyalty to the emperor a legal obligation of every soldier, as well as a spiritual endeavor. An often-quoted phrase from the rescript tied together duty, death, disgrace, and dishonor: "Bear in mind that duty is weightier than a mountain, while death is lighter than a feather. Never by failing in moral principle fall into disgrace and bring dishonor upon your name." This was interpreted in ensuing years to mean that duty is a deep, absolute obligation; death is nothing for the soldier to face, so he should willingly give up his life if necessary. Moreover, disgrace and dishonor would smear the name and the family of anyone who failed his commitment. The greatest disgrace awaited those who retreated or surrendered. This resulted in a tradition of "death rather than surrender."[6]

At the start of World War II, General Hideki Tojo made it clear in the <u>Senjinkun</u> (Soldier's Code) that a soldier who surrendered to become a prisoner of war should be ashamed for trying to prolong his own life. His duty was to kill or be killed. Any Japanese prisoner of war recaptured after having surrendered would face a court martial and certain punishment. Soldiers were also told that Americans tortured and killed prisoners of war.

Any behavior that hinted at cowardice came under severe discipline. Ivan Morris describes the plight of six kamikaze pilots who were given the traditional send-off celebration with farewell toasts of sake upon departing on their glorious suicide mission. But the weather that day was poor, with heavy cloud cover. Targeted American ships could not be located, and the mission commander decided to return to his base to await another day. Because they returned, the pilots were ridiculed for wasting their precious fuel, insulted as "contemptible cowards," and each slapped in the face (a symbolically demoralizing blow.) They were given menial duties to perform. They were made to feel worthless and, in fact, did assume a worthless state of mind.[8]

Of the Japanese, British General William Slim,

campaigning in Burma, said, "Everyone talks about fighting to the last man and last round, but only the Japanese <u>actually do it</u>." [9]

The army taught discipline to soldiers by both physical and spiritual means. Superiors beat recruits to instill obedience to orders. Numerous sources relate the woeful experiences of recruits unmercifully beaten for minor infractions. The psychology of such situations, neatly termed the "transfer of oppression", describes a scenario wherein those in relatively inferior positions felt suppressed and projected those feelings upon their inferiors, who in turn directed their oppression to those below them.[10]   Military organizations, where absolute obedience is required, are prone to such oppression.

The army also carried out a program of "spiritual education" as a continuation of the morals classes conducted in the public schools. Although Confucianism and its advocacy of filial piety formed an integral part of the nation's culture, the Japanese schools taught that filial piety ranked below loyalty to the emperor. The Chinese believed loyalty to family came first.[11]

The Japanese owed the greatest of <u>on</u> (a feeling of a deep indebtedness for benevolences extended) to the emperor. Children were taught that their birth and the care given to them by their parents became a debt to be repaid over one's lifetime. The emperor reigned as the benevolent father of the whole nation, so the greatest <u>on</u> was owed to him.[12]

The army reinforced loyalty to the Emperor and strongly emphasized the Five Articles of the Imperial Rescript to Soldiers and Sailors:

(1) A soldier must do his duty to his country.

(2) A soldier must be courteous.

(3) A soldier must show courage in war.

(4) A soldier must keep his word.

(5) A soldier must live simply.

Additionally, officers received instruction in the samurai code, which required loyalty, valor, and total commitment. They proudly carried swords and assumed the role of samurai warriors. Although not part of army regulations, the samurai code existed as an ideal to be followed.[13]

One uniquely Japanese method which officers used to discipline individual troops involved a simple threat to write home to the soldier's parents expressing disappointment at their son's poor performance, or failure to fulfill his duty.[14]   Ruth Benedict's discussion of cultures where shame is the major sanction does much to explain the feelings of Japanese soldiers who were openly ridiculed or criticized.[15]   The recalcitrant soldier, or a soldier who failed in his mission, would feel deep shame and acute personal chagrin.

During General Masaharu Homma's campaign in the Philippines, problems with inadequate supplies and personnel caused delays in his advances.   The general received a message from the imperial headquarters which said, "The Emperor is very concerned about your strategic situation. Why are you making no progress?" This seemingly straightforward question became a most humiliating experience for the general and he was seen to weep openly.[16]

Former Private Yuji Aida (who later became a professor of history at Kyoto University) surrendered to the British when the war was declared over. He was categorized among the "surrendered personnel," an important distinction as compared to "Prisoners of War" who were captured during the hostilities. Aida's unit followed orders and surrendered as a result of Japan's acceptance of the Potsdam Declaration. They did not suffer the personal humiliation of the prisoners of war. While in a detention camp awaiting repatriation, Aida saw some Japanese troops who were captured as prisoners of war. He described their mental state:

> They were Japanese in soldiers' uniforms, doing the
> same work as ourselves, who avoided us and did not
> talk to us . . . I said 'hello' to one of them but he
> turned away and would not talk to me.... You could
> see how powerful was the indoctrination of the
> Japanese Army. Even after the war, these '
> prisoners of war ' were convinced that we despised
> them and so they kept themselves aloof, on the
> defensive. They were ashamed of themselves.[17]

Along with obedience and spiritual training, rugged
physical endurance marches, samurai spirited officers,
and a culture of shame overshadowing their movements,
Japanese soldiers also received positive reinforcement
for giving their lives for the emperor. Their names would
be listed at the Yasukuni Shrine in Tokyo, and they
would be worshipped as gods, an honor only bestowed
upon national heroes. Dying for the emperor and being
enshrined at Yasukuni would bring fame to their family
name and thus fulfill the obligations of filial piety.[18]

Aida, a college instructor when inducted, did not
looking forward to dying. He confessed to feeling
ashamed because he had been cunning, while other

soldiers who were unskilled at dodging, hiding, or loafing went uncomplaining to their deaths.   "The sort of people who suffer most in times like these," he said, "are people who are slow to think and act, comparatively honest and unable to do anything outstanding.   These decent, solid types were always more numerous among the men than among the officers and NCOs and so most of them [in his unit] had been killed." [19]

Lieutenant Onoda represented a typical graduate of army training, the morals classes of his youth, and state Shinto.   When he completed officers' school and received his orders in 1944, he determined to remain true to them.   He remembered well the words of encouragement given his unit by Lieutenant General Akira Muto when they received their assignment. "It is urgent that you exert every effort to carry out your orders," the general had said. "It may take three years, it may take five, but whatever happens, we'll come back for you. until then, so long as you have one soldier, you are to continue to lead him. You may have to live on coconuts. If that's the case, live on coconuts!   Under no circumstances are you to give up your life voluntarily."[20]

It was clear in the new lieutenant's mind that in

being sent to the island of Lubang, about 350 miles southwest of Manila, he was undertaking an important mission. Although officers' training school taught Onoda not to think but to lead troops in battle, resolved to die if necessary, the special training he received in guerilla warfare prepared him to stay alive and fight as long as possible, even if this meant resorting to conduct normally considered disgraceful.   Intelligence gathering behind enemy lines, camouflage, and survival techniques were part of the training. As a "guerilla" there was integrity in secret warfare, he was told. It was even permissible to be taken prisoner and to give the enemy false information.[21]

Not that Hiroo Onoda expected that would happen. With the example in mind of his older brother who was serving in Shanghai, he was ready to be a guerilla in the mountains until he died there.   "Although I knew that my struggle would bring me neither fame nor honor, I did not care," he said later. "I was prepared to die.   If it is of the slightest use to my country, I shall be happy," he thought. [22]

During the Allied struggle to regaln the Philippines in July 1944, there was limited action on Lubang.   The

United States Navy pounded the island's shores with a heavy artillery bombardment. American troops established a beachhead and the Japanese garrison there was quickly subdued. Onoda and several other soldiers were in the mountains where they could see the battle for the small town below. They realized that the Japanese were defeated on Lubang, but expected a relief force to land and recapture the island. There was no order to surrender and no reason to do so. The enemy did not know their whereabouts. The thick vegetation covered their trail so Onoda and the few soldiers with him could move inland easily. Thinking of his duty, Onoda devoted his efforts toward being ready for the return of Japanese forces. For thirty years, he mentally prepared many reports to turn over to the returning imperial forces whenever they might arrive.

The experiences of Ito and Minagawa (sixteen years) and Yokoi (twenty-eight years) were similar. Ito was told by officer Cadet Asada during the battle for Guam Ito and Minagawa relied on each other for support, growing closer as the years passed, but waiting for a counterattack by Japanese troops. "In the matter of morale, the one means left to us was to sustain each other by a joint concentration on the single rallying point of the relieving force from Japan; and on the objective of staying alive until that landing force should appear," said Ito. Yokoi did not have a companion. He literally became a recluse, living in his own cave, and ready to spend his life there rather than surrender.

Initially they were separated from the main units on Guam and became isolated. Action quieted, but the presence of so many Americans told them that the island had been lost. There was no thought of surrender, only remorse because they could not die gloriously for the emperor. They too decided to wait for the return of the Japanese army. Another reason they may have stayed hidden was because they feared facing other Japanese who would accuse them of not having fought to the death.[23]

The stragglers' days were filled with a quest for food. They searched for anything edible, including roots, breadfruit, coconuts, bananas, shrimp, eels, and an occasional chicken, cow, or deer. Yokoi relates how he caught a rat, skinned and cooked it. Often there was nothing to eat. Hunger became an almost constant companion. They found or fashioned their own tools and took great care of the few weapons and what

ammunition they had.   They took pains to stay under
cover, use camouflage, and avoid being captured.

The native Guamanian tribesmen, with their jungle
knowledge, were more dangerous to the Japanese than
the Americans and Australians. The native hunters
tracked silently and fired without warning. Ito suffered a
superficial bullet wound across his back in a surprise
encounter. Only a quick dive into thick foliage saved his
life. Ito and Minagawa moved their base camps often;
Yokoi hid in a dark, underground cave with a carefully
concealed entrance. Although Ito and Minagawa were
close to the upper reaches of the Talofofo River, near
Yokoi's cave, they did not meet.

Each of their stories was chronicled in detail by the
Japanese media, which fed an insatiable public with the
exploits of these soldiers when they finally were
returned to Japan. Ito and Minagawa returned in May
1960 as heroes, thronged by crowds of well-wishers
everywhere. Their spirit as determined soldiers was
widely admired.   One welcoming banner proclaimed,
"Congratulations, Sergeant Ito!   Long live patriotism
like yours!" Press conferences, interviews and the
general reaction overwhelmed them. They returned as

living symbols of the Japanese warrior spirit.

That spirit was rekindled again In 1972 when Yokoi was captured. Takie Lebra provides insight into the feelings of the general public: "The nation-wide excitement about the discovery of Sergeant Yokoi seems compounded by the guilt aroused in many Japanese through their vicarious retroexperience of his deprivation and loneliness. They may also have felt proud of his endurance and unswerving Japanese loyalty."[24]

As a guerilla, Onoda was more active than Yokoi. He and three others he led fired upon the villagers of Lubang to steal their rice or kill their cattle. The presence of the small band became known, and they were hunted through the hills by the local constabulary and the Philippine army. Disease and malnutrition claimed the life of one of Onoda's band. Another was killed by return fire. The last soldier to endure with Onoda was Private First Class Kinshichi Kozuka, killed in 1972 in a skirmish with the local police.[25]

The Japanese government and the relatives of these army stragglers made efforts over the years to contact them and to convince them to come out of hiding. Officials and family members went to the islands with postwar pictures and newspapers. They searched, used loudspeakers to call into the jungle, and left messages. One leaflet found by Ito and Minagawa showed a picture of the Emperor meeting MacArthur, with the message:

"The war is over. The Japanese Army has surrendered unconditionally and a meeting has taken place between the Supreme Commander, MacArthur, and the Emperor of Japan. This is no deception and no trap and Japanese military personnel should assemble without anxiety or concern at the Reception Centre at Agana, on the northern coast of Guam, where arrangements will be made to facilitate their early return to Japan."

They threw it away, refusing to believe it. Years later Minagawa explained, "Yes, we saw the leaflets all right. But we were convinced that they were spurious and were meant as a trap. None of us believed they were genuine."

The Asahi Shimbun sponsored a small plane trailing a banner flying over the jungle with a message to the stragglers to come out. But all these efforts were in vain. Onoda saw the newspaper's plane but decided he would not be fooled by a trick like that! The army's indoctrination had been too effective. The soldiers feared an enemy trap. They could not believe that the war was over. The stragglers refused to face the humiliation of surrender. "I sincerely believed that Japan would not surrender so long as one Japanese remained alive," Onoda said.[26] "I had been taught that the war might last a hundred years.   I had received special orders directly from a lieutenant general, who had assured me that eventually the Japanese Army would come after me, no matter how long it might take. "[27]

Minagawa and Ito were captured after sixteen years on Guam; Yokoi after twenty-eight years. They were incredulous at the kind treatment they received.   They were fed, given medical examinations and care, barbered, and clothed. But they expected to be killed by their American captors at any moment.   Not until they returned to the homeland did they truly believe the war was over.

A young Japanese adventurer, Norio Suzuki, had read reports of an army straggler fighting on in the Philippines. He decided to go to Lubang in 1974 to search for him. Suzuki camped alongside a river bordering the jungle and within a few days was spotted by Onoda, who realized Suzuki was not an island native. Onoda cautiously made contact.   Wary as only a man who has escaped captivity for thirty years could be,

Onoda did not trust what Suzuki told him. His orders had not been rescinded and that meant the army high command wanted him to stay on the island.[28] "No," Onoda said, he would not come out until he heard from Major Taniguchi, his commanding officer. Onoda did not think that would happen. That was the key point to Onoda. But it did happen.

Suzuki returned to Japan and, with the assistance of the government, found Major Yoshimi Taniguchi. In February 1974, Taniguchi, who was then managing a bookstore in Miyazaki Prefecture, traveled to Lubang and made contact with Onoda. There, in the jungle, a last official function of the Japanese Imperial Army was held. The major read Lieutenant Onoda a letter written by General Tomoyuki Yamashita, who had been the supreme commander of Japanese forces in the Philippines, ordering the surrender. Taniguchi also read Onoda a letter of his own.[29] With his new orders Onoda's war had ended. The final Japanese army straggler surrendered. In a ceremony the next day, Onoda handed over to a Philippine general the sword he had preserved immaculately for thirty years. The general accepted Onoda's surrender and magnanimously returned the sword to him.

Upon leaving Lubang, the dazed Onoda reflected, "Why had I fought here for thirty years? Who had I been fighting for? What was the cause?"[30]

The motivation of these soldiers was based upon their upbringing in a society that worshipped the emperor, taught loyalty to the empire in the schools, and used the samurai code to drill obedience and the shame of surrender into them as soldiers. This strong mental conditioning gave them the will to overcome the isolation and physical deprivation of the jungle. Each of these stragglers returned to Japan with a deep sense of shame. They had lost the war and carried with them a heavy burden of failure. They wanted to visit the families of their comrades who had died; they sought to pray at the Yasukuni Shrine for the souls of those who were killed. Their belief in the Shinto religion and their mission as soldiers remained with them even as they acknowledged defeat. They still worshipped the Emperor.

Although their training was based on a prewar model and represented militaristic concepts that were labeled anachronistic in the postwar period, the public welcomed these returnees as heroes. The ubiquitous Japanese media detailed the stories of the stragglers for days.   Yokoi had been a sergeant, a good soldier Schweik, but barely literate.   The <u>Asahi Shimbun</u>, a major nationally circulated newspaper whose reporters were among the first on the scene in Guam, assigned a team to interview him and put the story into book form. Yokoi's memoir, <u>Asu E no Michi</u> (The Road to Tomorrow), was on the national best seller list when Onoda surrendered in March 1974.

In Onoda, an officer who understood and believed the military code, a modest, but articulate national hero emerged.   To meet the demand for news of his story, Onoda held press conferences and gave interviews.   He was lionized by crowds everywhere and bewildered by it all.   The press covered the emotional meeting with his aged parents, his nineteen-day hospital checkup, a solemn visit to Yasukuni Shrine, a meeting with Prime Minister Kakuei Tanaka, what his pension benefits would be, the reinstatement of his name in the family register, comments from his former classmates, and more.   He received fan mail from throughout the country, including many offers of marriage.[31] In his autobiography Onoda describes with shock the advances made by one war widow who sought to capture him as a husband.   Eventually he did choose a bride and started a new life as the director of a children's nature camp in northern Japan.

By paying his respects to the souls of the war dead at Yasukuni Shrine, Onoda did much to encourage their remembrance. Each year on August 15th thousands of mourners make a pilgrimage to Yasukuni. They are also encouraged by the powerful Association of Bereaved Families, with a membership of more than one million households. Then Prime Minister Ryutaro Hashimoto, was a former head of the organization, instrumental in 1995 in blocking a Diet resolution which would have apologized for the war. Although Yasukuni is identified with Japanese militarism, Government officials visit the shrine in a "private" capacity.

Certainly, the stragglers were men of courage and bravery. Their motivation took years from their lives in devotion to a lost cause. Admirable, tragic, but at the same time the kind of heroes the Japanese loved: devoted, solitary warriors who bowed their heads and faithfully followed the narrow path that was their call to duty.

Yokoi and Onoda's reception as heroes, occurring amidst the economic prosperity of the 1970s and the democratic government the Japanese embraced, startled most observers. The ghosts of militarism past had not died; the embers of the spirit, smoldering beneath the national surface, were rekindled.   For the Self-Defense Forces Lt. Onoda's return provided the best example of the power of spiritual training (seishin kyoiku). The SDF had struggled in the postwar era to maintain its stature as a formidable military organization. The attitude of the public, the purpose of the forces, the constitutionality of the SDF, and the motivation of the troops were all being questioned.   Capt. Saizo Nagatomo of the Air Defense Force wrote, "the first problem we face is coming up with a contemporary spiritual equivalent to the shining samurai spirit that undergirded the prewar army."   The result became a new sense of mission to replace the blind loyalty to the Emperor with a responsibility for service to the nation.[32]

Military commentator Osamu Inagaki considered the SDF's new ideology merely an attempt to hide the true feelings of unrepentant militarists. Inagaki pointed out that in an award winning essay contest for Air Force cadets, Capt. Yoshinori Higuchi had written, "No human organization can move forthrightly toward the achievement of its goals while at the same time harboring internal spiritual contradictions. The SDF is no exception . . . The simplest solution to this problem is to remove one of the conflicting alternatives. In the case of the Jietai, this would mean eradicating the democratic spirit and promoting the ways of totalitarianism."[33]

Admiration for the old values did not die easily. Even the Emperor's name became entangled in the SDF's new mission when Keikichi Masuhara, director general of the Defense Agency, told reporters that the Emperor had privately told him of his support for the national defense forces. Within a few days of this report, on May 29, 1973, Masuhara was force to resign and thus protect the name of the Emperor.

Lt. Onoda's story appeared in the news again in May 1996 when the Philippine Government, eager to promote investment and tourism by the Japanese, invited him to tour Lubang and revisit his old lair in the jungle. Still recalling his role as a wartime guerilla, Onoda initially refused the invitation but was later convinced by Philippine officials that the island natives harbored no resentment against him.

For the Japanese nation the event became another opportunity to admire a warrior who represented his country as a samurai.

Notes - Chapter 4

1. Kiyoaki Murata, "The War Saga Boom," Japan Times (8 Dec. 1956).

2. Kiyoaki Murata, "Blood and Tears," Japan Times (3 Aug. 1957) .

3. Hiroo Onoda, No Surrender, My Thirty-Year War (Tokyo: Kodansha International Ltd., 1979), 201.

4. Hillis Lory, Japan's Military Masters (New York: The Viking Press, 1943), 40.

5. Ibid.

6. Lory, 81.

7. Ibid., 16.

8. Ivan Morris, The Nobility of Failure (New York: Holt, Rinehart and Winston), 323-326.

9. Arthur Swinson, Four Samurai (London: Hutchinson & Co., 1968), 17.

10. Kazuko Tsurumi, Social Change and the Individual (Princeton: Princeton University Press, 1970), 95.

11. Ronald S. Anderson, Japan, Three Epochs of Modern Education (Washington, D.C.: U.S. Department of

Health, Education, and Welfare, 1959), 3.

12. Tsurumi, 93. See: Benedict, "Schematic Table of Japanese Obligations and Their Reciprocals," The Chrysanthemum and the Sword, 116.

13. Swinson, 15.

14. Lory, 65.

15. Ruth Benedict, The Chrysanthemum and the Sword (Boston: Houghton Mifflin Co., 1946), 222-224.

16. Swinson, 62.

17. Yuji Aida, Prisoner of the British (London: The Cresset Press, 1966), 50.

18. Tsurumi, 125.

19. Aida, 21.

20. Onoda, 43-44.

21. Ibid., 33.

22. Ibid., 36.

23. Takie Sugiyama Lebra, Japanese Patterns of Behavior (Honolulu: University of Hawaii Press, 1976), 14.

24.   Ibid. ,36.

25.   Ibid. ,174.

26.   Ibid. ,118.

27.   Ibid. ,125.

28.   Ibid. ,208.

29. "Onoda's Former Superior Confident of Success,"
Japan Times (1 March 1974), 2.

30. Ibid., 219.

31. Japan Times (Feb. 27 to Mar. 31, 1974). There were
almost daily news stories, including page one banner
headlines, to mark his surrender and his return to Japan
on March 12.

32. Inagaki, Osamu. "The Jietai: Military Values in a
Pacifist Society." The Japan Interpreter (Summer, 1975),
1-15.

33.Ibid., 14.

Chapter 5

YUKIO MISHIMA AS A SAMURAI

By the time Yukio Mishima finished speaking to the assembled soldiers at the Ichigaya army compound on November 25, 1970, he must have realized his mission was lost. He faced a futile effort trying to convince the Japanese Self-Defense Force to rebel and show their loyalty to the Emperor. Communications were poor: his shouts from a second floor balcony could barely be heard. The talk was disjointed and the young troops did not understand what he was talking about. When they did understand, Mishima heard his audience jeering him. Undaunted, he continued with his speech, finished with "Tenno Heika Banzai!" (Long Live the Emperor!) and then withdrew to disembowel himself. Along with one of his followers in the Shield Society (Tate no Kai), often referred to as his private army, Mishima committed seppuku.

"One part of my mind still kept on telling me that it was now futile to perform this deed, but my new-found strength had no fear of futility. I must do the deed precisely because it was so futile. "[1] These words fit

Mishima's act of self destruction, but they were actually what Mishima wrote to describe the thoughts of the acolyte Mizoguchi in <u>The Temple of the Golden Pavilion</u>. In setting fire to the temple, Mizoguchi had freed himself from a dark, foreboding existence, attaining self-fulfillment for the first time in his life even though he knew the act was futile.

By sacrificing his life to the ultranationalist cause of devotion to the Emperor, Mishima reached his own fulfillment, completing a lifetime effort to achieve a measure of heroic stature.

The general public and his millions of admirers could not imagine that Mishima seriously expected to effect a metamorphosis of the Japanese national character by disemboweling himself in the samurai manner. Did he know then that the act was futile? After a lifetime of literary achievement, including consideration for the Nobel prize in literature, the intellectual acumen embodied within Mishima was unlikely to be deceived. He was surely aware that outside of the <u>Tate no Kai</u> and a few other fringe ultranationalist groups there was little public sentiment for a strengthening of imperial powers.

By November 1970 advancing consumerism and

income-doubling economic expansion had caught the fancy of the country. It was a time of rapid technological progress and of unprecedented economic growth, with per capita income approaching European levels and aggregate output exceeding that of all countries but the United States and the Soviet Union. The Japanese were looking forward to buying cars, to enjoying electronic appliances, and to saving for homes. They did not wish to be reminded of the past excesses of the Imperial Japanese Army.

Mishima knew all this. In the final statement he left for the press, he criticized postwar Japan as "a spiritual vacuum, preoccupied only with its economic prosperity, unmindful of its national foundations, losing its national spirit, seeking trivialities without looking to fundamentals, and falling into makeshift expediency and hypocrisy."[2]

Mishima's seppuku raised the specter of Japanese militarism, an unpopular cause and a source of embarrassment for the Japanese then as now.   What then was the basis and meaning of Mishima's final act? What was its relevance in relation to the samurai code?

The act of seppuku is validated in the samurai code, which is based primarily on unswervlng loyalty to one's master. A failure to perform one's duty or the assumption of responsibility for an event were the major reasons for seppuku. The code also recognized it as the ultimate sacrifice by an underling who wished to follow his master in death, or who attempted to call attention to his master's mistaken ways.   By a strict definition of the code, Mishima's seppuku did not meet any of these conditions.   Who was his master?   For what event was he responsible?   Who was he admonishing when he criticized the errant ways of the Japanese?

Mishima's interpretation of the code, as presented In Hagakure Nyumon (The Way of the Samurai), showed that he knew the samurai ethic intimately. Indeed, it had become a part of his daily life.   He saw it as showing guiding principles for human beings in certain fixed conditions--as universal teachings with practical knowledge based on practical experience.[3] Mishima's own path to becoming a samurai is perhaps best explained in Sun & Steel, an autobiographical account of training for physical and mental strength and discipline.

I cherished a romantic impulse toward death, yet at the same time I required a strictly classical body as

its vehicle; a peculiar sense of destiny made me
believe that the reason why my romantic impulse
toward death remained unfulfilled in reality was the
immensely simple fact that I lacked the necessary
physical qualifications . . . Any confrontation
between weak, flabby flesh and death seemed to me
absurdly inappropriate. Longing at eighteen for an
early demise, I felt myself unfitted for it.   I lacked,
in short, the muscles suitable for a dramatic death.
And it deeply offended my romantic pride that it
should be this unsuitability that had permitted me to
survive the war.[4]

Matthew Ikeda, in a psychological study of
Mishima, finds Mishima's reaction to Japan's defeat in
the Pacific war "highly complex and ambivalent."
Preoccupied as Mishima was with the concept of a
romantic and erotic death, one replete with the aesthetics
of youth, "his failure to die a hero's death for the
Emperor like so many of his courageous peers was to
remain as a latent and unique source of psychological
and existential conflict associated with the loss of
adolescence."[5]

As a youth Mishima's well-to-do family carefully
supervised his upbringing. A doting, possessive

grandmother, along with the rest of the family, sought to shelter him because of his weak, sickly body. His childhood was restricted to playing indoors at the side of his grandmother. His playmates were few and specially selected. Although lonely, he was not dull. His grandmother took him to kabuki and noh plays. He read avidly, including Japanese classics and translations of foreign writers, and found joy in making up his own stories. A brilliant student, he finished at the top of his class at the prestigious Gakushuin Middle School and received a silver watch from the Emperor as a reward. His literary bent was shaped early, but his physical prowess was almost nil.   At age 19, when he had already written several pieces for publication, he received his draft notice.[6]

In the autobiographical Confessions of a Mask, Mishima recalled failing the army physical examination in a rural area where his family maintained their legal residence.

My father's theory was that my weak physique would attract more attention in a rural area than in the city, where such weakness was no rarity, and that as a result I would probably not be drafted. As a

matter of fact, I had provided the examining
officials with cause for an outbreak of laughter
when I could not lift--not even as far as my
chest--the bale of rice that the farm boys were easily
lifting above their heads ten times.[7]

On the day of the examination, in February 1945,
Mishima had a cold and fever, leading the doctor who
examined him to conclude that there was a chest rattle,
an indication of incipient tuberculosis. Mishima
confessed that he lied, telling the doctor that the fever
was a lingering one of over six months and that he spit
blood and had night sweats. When ordered home as unfit
for service Mishima admitted that he "felt the pressure of
a smile come pushing" to his lips.[8]

The war ended six months later. Mishima's
biographers do not suggest that he objected to the war on
ideological grounds, only that he was influenced by his
family's wishes and his own physical weakness. At a
time when young recruits sought death to express their
loyalty to the Emperor, Mishima too dreamed of a
glorious demise, but not for the same reason. His desire
was to die as a "beautiful martyr", a dream shattered
when Japan surrendered.[9] Years later, writing about the

suicide squadrons of kamikaze pilots, Mishima said, "The spirit of those young men who for the sake of their country hurled themselves to certain death is closest in the long history of Japan to the clear ideal of action and death offered in <u>Hagakure</u>."[10]

Mishima remained physically weak until he was thirty years old.   In 1955 when he was being acclaimed as a major Japanese author, he met Hitoshi Tamari, the coach of Waseda University's physical culture club, and began a program of bodybuilding.   After a year of thrice-weekly weightlifting workouts, Mishima confessed,

> I could hardly believe my eyes. I saw the apparently miraculous proof of what the flesh, which had seemed in my youth so unresponsive to the spirit in which all my dependence lay, had now been able to accomplish under the force of that spirit.[11]

Chronic stomach problems disappeared as his body gained strength.

During that period, he also reflected on the interrelationship of body and mind, and concluded that as a writer a less than healthy view of the world was an asset. A critical, questioning mind would be beneficial, and the way to protect that mindset would be to keep the flesh in the best possible shape. As he gained strength, he also gained confidence in his body. He then turned to the world of sport, which he had not participated in before.[12] Mishima began training for boxing, but soon realized that was beyond his powers at age thirty. As a substitute, he took up the martial art of kendo, a form of swordsmanship, that as a schoolboy had offended his sensibilities. He now enjoyed the rough, slashing interplay and deep, guttural cries of competitive action. A screaming "eeeyyaahhh!" combined with a forceful thrust to maximize one's energy became a delight.

> The sound is pleasant to me; I have fallen in love with it. This sound is the cry of Nippon itself buried deep within me. . . It is a cry that present-day Nippon is ashamed of and desperately tries to suppress. . . . It is something bound up with memories that are dark, something that recalls the flow of new-shed blood. But whatever the recollections it provokes, they are the ones that most truthfully recall our nation's past. It is the cry of our race bursting through the shell of modernization. [13]

Physically Mishima was described as "a

picture-story illustration of the high correlation . ..
found between physique and temperament." In his
youth Mishima was considered ectomorphic, sickly,
and lean. In Ikeda's study he was seen as having a
temperament called cerebrotonia: "restraint in
posture and movement, love of privacy, mental
overintensity, introversion, need of solitude when
troubled, and an orientation toward the later periods
of life. . . . The Mishima of the 1960s was a
possessor of a powerful mesomorphic physique."
There was an extremely high correlation between
his new physique and a somototonian temperament,
characterized by "assertiveness of posture and
movement, love of physical adventure, love of
domination, love of risk and chance, physical
courage for combat, Spartan indifference to pain . . .
extroversion, need of action when troubled, and an
orientation toward the goals and activities of
youth."[14]

From age thirty, kendo and bodybuilding became a
way of life for Mishima, incorporated into his daily
routine along with his writing.   He would rise at noon,
work out physically in the afternoon, dine and attend the
theater or some other event in the evening, and then

return home to write through the night. He often visited the exclusive Clark Hatch Physical Fitness Center in Azabu, Tokyo, where he could practice his English with the foreign businessmen there while lifting weights. Two days before his death he went through a bodybuilding routine at the center accompanied by two students from Kanagawa University, presumably members of the Tate no Kai.[15]

His physical maturity and stature as a prominent author allowed Mishima to be his own man and to perform as he wished: to pose nude as a photographer's model, to play leading roles as a movie actor, and to appear as a voice for the right wing.

"Patriotism," a short story which he wrote in 1960, is a precursor of Mishima's own seppuku. He later starred in the movie version of the story. It is based loosely on the aborted rebellion of February 26, 1936. By committing seppuku Lieutenant Shinji Takeyama assumed responsibility for the actions of the men under his command who had revolted. The lieutenant had been married less than six months at the time. The tale was one of honor, morality, and love with exquisite detail in the sensuous feelings in the couple's final act of love and the careful preparations for the disembowelment.[16]

From their first night of marriage the lieutenant had instructed his young wife, Reiko, in the ways of a soldier, the discipline that he, and she as his wife, must follow. He told her to be ready for his death at any time.   When that moment finally comes, Mishima's characters follow the admonishment given in Hagakure: "If you are slain with an unseemly appearance, you will show lack of previous resolve, will be despised by your enemy and will appear unclean."[17]   Reiko assists her husband with his bath, pleases him with her uninhibited love-making and then helps him prepare for his suicide.   The young wife witnesses her husband's seppuku, then dutifully follows him by piercing her throat.   There is a vivid description of the death scenes, gory but almost clinical in detail.   The lieutenant leaves a farewell note of one sentence: "Long live the Imperial Forces." [18]

Henry Scott-Stokes believes Mishima rehearsed his own death in "Patriotism" and other works containing belly cutting sequences. In Runaway Horses the protagonist, a rightwing terrorist, commits seppuku.   In 1969 Mishima played the role of a samurai who commits seppuku in the film Hitogiri.[19]

At the same time that "Patriotism" appeared, another

magazine published "Seventeen" by Kenzaburo Oe, a noted contemporary of Mishima's who would go on to win a Nobel prize for literature. Oe's fictional hero was a seventeen-year-old who became an ardent rightist and found fulfillment in devoting his life to the Emperor.[20] Oe knew well of the parallel between his work and Mishima's. During an interview when asked about the samurai spirit in postwar Japan, Oe immediately responded, "Oh, Mishima," pausing but leaving no doubt of the first thought that came to his mind: the strong image of Mishima as a samurai.[21]

Mishima clearly separated the personal and professional areas of his life. When he was married in 1958, one of the conditions of the o-miai (an arranged meeting of prospective marital candidates) was that he required time alone in a private setting to do his work and that his betrothed was never to interfere. Accounts of their life together indicate that his wife, Yoko, did not know of his plans for seppuku.

Mishima had traveled abroad and had a good knowledge of English. He was acquainted with many in the foreign community in Tokyo and enjoyed a close, personal relationship with a select few. Edward Seidensticker found it enigmatic that while Mishima "enjoyed the company of foreigners and lived the life style of a Westernized dandy, his final act made

Mishima an unregenerate believer in the Japanese martial spirit."[22]

During the 1950s Mishima's writings did not reflect his political opinions, although he clearly did not care for the "liberal" movement among Japanese intellectuals. His view was that "now if ever was the time for reviving the old Japanese ideal of a combination of letters and the martial arts, of art and action." [23]

Mishima's imagination was fired by the fierce demonstrations in 1960 opposing the United States-Japan Security Treaty[24] and by the assassination of Socialist Party Chairman Inejiro Asanuma by a young rightist. Asanuma was stabbed with a short sword, the traditional weapon of Japanese terrorists, while giving a speech. In 1968 Mishima was asked what he thought of the assassin and replied, "He was splendid. As you know, he took his own life afterward. In dying that way (he hanged himself in jail) he was being faithful to the letter of Japanese tradition."[25] Taking his own life displayed the "sincerity" of the act, a factor that can be related to Mishima's own suicide.

Mishima's impressions of the anti-security treaty movement of 1960 would later influence his actions in 1970, when the treaty would be extended. His interest in the movement was analytical. He observed the emotions of the protesters and the way they did battle with the police using rocks and staves. He did not share the students' and socialists' fears that the Security Treaty would make Japan the battleground in a world war, nor did he object to Japan's rearmament.

Mishima's own views, which became clear during the sixties, were that the prewar respect for the Emperor should be restored, that the constitution should be amended to allow Japan to rearm, and that the Self-Defense Forces (SDF) should become the Japanese Imperial Army of days gone by. In his essay "The Defense of Culture" he said that Japanese culture included the chrysanthemum, the sword, martial arts, bushido,

> and even (or perhaps particularly) terrorism. . . . Since the ultimate source of the honor of the chrysanthemum and the sword is the Emperor, military honor must also proceed from the Emperor. Supreme command must be restored to him. . . . It is urgent that the Emperor and the army be linked with bonds of honor.[26]

Mishima was particularly irked by the restricted role

allowed to the SDF whose very existence was denied by the constitution. It is, he said, the

> unfortunate nature of Japan's foundling army that deliberately keeps it far removed from any ideas of tradition or glory. The power it generates is never used for any effective purpose. Everything is devoted to the enormous hypothesis of a 'coming war'. . . The vacuum in which nothing happens progresses from day to day. [27]

Mishima's opinion of the SDF was based in part on personal experience and knowledge.   In 1966 Mishima requested and received permission to train with the army at training grounds near Mt. Fuji. He was also given access to the Air Self-Defense Force and taken up in a jet aircraft.   When he organized the Tate no Kai in 1967, his recruits, drawn from within the membership of an existing rightist group, were also allowed to train at the army camp, and did so annually thereafter.[28]

The Tate no Kai was formed, he explained, "in the determination to sacrifice our lives in order to make of the Self-Defense Forces, when it awakens, a national army, an honorable national army."[29] It was to be a militia, trained in guerilla operations and intelligence activities.   Membership, by invitation only, grew to about 100, mostly university students who had shown rightwing leanings and the proper Japanese attitude. Mishima supported it financially, wrote its charter, and was the group`s field leader and spokesman. "Inferior as I am to the task," he said, "I am simply rekindling the dying embers of Japan`s warrior spirit." [30]

Mishima had become his own samurai, committed to the Emperor, the revision of the constitution, and the re- establishment of the military honor of the Japanese army. He now regretted his weakness as a youth which had caused him to miss the war.

> How ironical it was! At a period when the futureless cup of catastrophe had been brimming over, I had not been given the qualifications for drinking from it. I had gone away, and when, after long training, I had returned armed with those qualifications in fullest measure, it was to find the cup drained, its bottom coldly visible, and myself past forty.[31]

The Japanese public did not take the Tate no Kai seriously. They regarded it as Mishima's private army. His support of the group was considered foolish, even by his friends.[32]

If Mishima had planned a coup in one of his novels, after the formation of a private army, the point had surely been reached to infiltrate the existing officer corps, follow that by gaining the complicity of a few well-placed ministers, and then to execute final plans for a military takeover.   The action would have been a logical progression of the plot.   The actual climax remains as enigmatic today as it was then.

Mishima placed much significance on the liberals' anti- Security Treaty movement in 1970.   He anticipated that there would be violence in opposition to the extension of the treaty and a resulting opportunity for revision of the constitution.   He wanted Japan to defend itself, not to rely on the United States.

Despite the leftist rhetoric leading up to that year, the demonstrations were comparatively uneventful. The government maintained much tighter control of the situation than it had in 1960, while the anti-treaty forces could not muster the same vigor they had earlier. Apathy affected the left as much as it did the right. Indeed, Mishima felt disappointed by the student strike at Tokyo

University in 1969, when the students took hostages but were overcome by riot police. He criticized the students. "When the final moment came, there was not one of them who believed in what he stood for sufficiently to hurl himself out of a window or fall on a sword."[33]

The cause of the Tate no Kai could only be advanced, Mishima thought, by taking action. "Because action often leads one close to death, once a person has left the contemplative life and entered the world of action, it is human nature that he must be enthralled by both the nihilism he feels in the face of death and a fateful mysticism."[34] In this vein, he conceived of a plan to take the commanding general at the Ichigaya army compound hostage and address the SDF troops. On November 25, 1970, he put his plan into action.

The only Westerner to witness his speech, historian Joyce C. Lebra, who was doing research at the army archives, described a hectic scene with soldiers hastily assembled, police warily entering the compound, and the press eagerly seeking a story. No one was sure what was happening. Mishima, resplendent in Tate no Kai uniform, began to shout from a balcony. He exhorted the soldiers "to rise in the name of the Emperor, to overthrow corrupt politicians and the Constitution and to create a genuine army. . . . Mishima's hoarse harangue was nearly drowned out by the shouts and jeers of his incredulous audience and by the noise of helicopters already circling overhead."[35]

He withdrew after seven minutes to complete the final scene.   In the captive general's office with his Tate no Kai cohorts as witnesses, Mishima proved his sincerity.   With his own treasured short sword he punctured his abdomen and cut across.   An ardent follower assisted by beheading Mishima to end his ordeal.   The seppuku was complete.

The government repudiated Mishima's act.   Prime Minister Eisaku Sato said, "He must have been crazy." Foreign newspapers warned of a resurgence of Japanese militarism. The Hong Kong newspaper Ta Kung Pao said Mishima's "hara-kiri" was "a bloody devilish performance to fan the mad Bushido spirit of aggression and showed the madness of Japan's extreme rightist reactionary forces that are working hard for the speedy revival of Japanese militarism."[36]   But there was no uprising and no appetite for one by the army or the general public.

The shock of Mishima's death resulted in headline news stories and a proliferation of magazine articles with explanations of his actions and personal reminiscences by the writers. The publicity caused a mini-boom in sales of Mishima's works. His publisher hastened to press with The Temple of Dawn, the third book in his tetralogy The Sea of Fertility, completed in the early morning hours of November 25.

Suicidologist Mamoru Iga explains Mishima's act as a result of a narcissistic temperament, involving a neurotic need for attention, and a strongly nourished feeling of amae (an attitude anticipating indulgence by others). "When his amae was not satisfied, the psychological damage he received was unusually strong." His view of an ideal society, militaristic and feudal, conflicted with reality. Narcissism and homosexuality also created a gap between his ego ideal and the real world. The manifest motive was kangen (remonstration) to a modern corrupt Japan. But Iga also sees it as an act of self-assertion displaying manhood, courage, and a return to traditional values, and to Japan's "glorius and powerful past."[37] Because Mishima' s reasons included group goals, conformity to tradition, and communication with other members of his group, his seppuku was described as an altruistic suicide in terms of Durkheim's typology.[38]

Ironically, since the rebirth of Japan's military forces in 1950, when General MacArthur had first ordered the creation of a 75,000-man police reserve, the SDF has grown vastly stronger. With a navy of some 300 ships (the fifth largest in the world) and an army of 180,000 well equipped soldiers, defense of the country had grown beyond just the main islands. Cutbacks in American defense spending and the prompting of the United States have induced Japan to assume more responsibility. Backed by enormous economic strength, Japan's military spending increased, defense boundaries expanded, and new equipment brought on line. The defense procurement budget was planned at near $10 billion for 1996, the largest for any non- nuclear nation at that time. Moreover, Japan increased the role of the Maritime SDF by extending its patrol range 1,000 miles eastward in the Pacific Ocean. The Air SDF was urged by defense contractors in the United States to modernize by purchasing America's jet fighters, considered the world's most advanced. However, rather than be tied to

American sources, at one time Japan decided to develop its own state-of-the-art fighter, the FS-X.   A joint Japan-U.S. effort later emerged. Japan was also invited to participate in the Strategic Defense Initiative (star wars). The capability of the SDF clearly has grown beyond defense but is legally limited to a peacekeeping role. In the years since Mishima's death the SDF has become a genuine military force, just as he wanted.

In a last letter to critic Donald Keene, Mishima wrote "I want to die as a samurai, rather than as a man of letters"[39] In the end he achieved the Confucian ideal of the complete man by being both a warrior and a scholar. Discussing the suicide of author Ryunosuke Akutagawa,   Mishima had once said: "Unfortunate is the writer whose personality rather than his art is still discussed long after his death."   He might easily have been speaking of himself.[40]

His death contained all the trappings of a samurai, following the set procedure carefully. Mishima had used the act of seppuku many times in his works, but in this instance, despite the shock value, it was not as convincing as he would have liked.

Notes - Chapter 5

1. Yukio Mishima, The Temple of the Golden Pavilion, trans. Ivan Morris (New York: Alfred A. Knopf, Inc., 1959),258.

2. Yukio Mishima, "An Appeal," trans. Harris I. Martin, The Japan Interpreter (Winter 1971),73.

3. Yukio Mishima, Hagakure Nyumon, trans. Kathryn Sparling (New York: Putnam Publishing Group, 1983), 40.

4. Yukio Mishima, Sun & Steel, trans. John Bester (Tokyo: Kodansha International Ltd., 1970), 27.

5. Matthew S. Ikeda, "Yukio Mishima: A Study of Personal Metamorphosis" (Ph.D. diss., University of Chicago, 1974), 59.

6. See John Nathan, Mishima, A Biography (Boston: Little, Brown and Co., 1974), and Henry Scott-Stokes, The Life and Death of Yukio Mishima (Toronto: Doubleday Canada, 1974).

7. Yukio Mishima, Confessions of a Mask, trans. Meredith Weatherby (New York: New Directions Publishing Co., 1958), 135.

8. Ibid., 136, 138.

9. Michiko Niikuni Wilson, "The Fabrication of Beauty:

The Art of Mishima Yukio" (Ph.D. diss., University of Texas, Austin, 1977), 44.

10. Mishima, <u>Way of the Samurai</u>, 101.

11. Yukio Mishima, "Testament of a Samurai," trans. Michael Gallagher, <u>Sports Illustrated</u> (11 Jan. 1971), 24.

12. Ibid., 25.

13. Ibid., 26.

14. Quoted in Ikeda, 84-85, from a study by William Sheldon, <u>The Varieties of Human Physique</u>.

15. Clark Hatch to Allan Wagner, 24 March 1990, personal correspondence.

16. Yukio Mishima, "Patriotism," trans. Geoffrey W. Sargent, <u>Esquire</u> (April 1966), 106- 107.

17. Yamamoto, 33.

18. Mishiima, "Patriotism," 106-107

19. Scott-Stokes, 26

20. Nathan, 182

21. Kenzaburo Oe, interview by author, San Diego, California, January 1990.

22. Edward Seidensticker, "Mishima Yukio," <u>Hudson</u>

Review (Summer 1971), 279.

23. Mishima, Sun & Steel, 49.

24. Scott-Stokes, 325.

25. Nathan, 184

26. Quoted in Nathan, 235

27. Mishima, Sun & Steel, 68

28. Scott- Stokes, 326.

29. Mishima, "An Appeal," 74.

30. Yukio Mishima, "Tate No Kai," trans. Andrew Horvat, Japan Interpreter (Winter 1971), 78.

31. Mishima, Sun & Steel, 62.

32. Scott-Stokes, 327

33. Quoted in Nathan, 248

34. Yukio Mishima, "Yang-Ming Thought as Revolutionary Philosophy," trans. Harris I. Martin, Japan Interpreter (Winter 1971), 81.

35. Joyce C. Lebra, "Mishima's Last Act," Literature East & West (Winter 1971), 280.

36. "Mishima's Act Hit by H'kong Paper," Japan Times (27 Nov. 1970), 1.

37. Mamoru Iga, The Thorn in the Chrysanthemum (Berkeley: University of California Press, 1986), 96, 100, 105-106.

38. Ibid., 9.

39.Quoted in Joyce C. Lebra, 283.

40.Beongcheon Yu, Akutagawa (Detroit: Wayne State University Press, 1972), 120, quoting from panel discussion "Akutagawa Ryunosuke and Modern Writers," Akutagawa Ryunosuke Annai, ed. Shinichiro Nakamura, vol. 20 (Tokyo: Iwanami, 1955).

Chapter 6

THE YAKUZA

Japanologists may consider it only a tenuous link between the historical samurai and the modern day yakuza, but there is little doubt that the heartfelt commitment embedded in such concepts as loyalty, duty, and bravery belong to both. The yakuza ties to the traditional samurai code have been transformed in the modified, present-day version to almost cult status. The code practiced assiduously by this criminal element has expanded to include guns along with their swords, and added stock manipulations to gambling as another source of income. The yakuza are also linked to the growing drug trade and gun-running.

As a relatively minor segment of Japan's population, the underworld yakuza represent a deviant manifestation of the samurai code. Their nefarious actions defile the chaste behavior described in <u>Hagakure</u>, or the heroics of real samurai, such as Takamori Saigo. But the link to the samurai is one that receives on-going public exposure as the yakuza gain publicity and recognition far beyond what their numbers would seemingly merit. They also exemplify the anomaly in Japan of a low frequency of individual crime along with the acknowledged existence of organized criminal groups.

Although the yakuza pre-date the 1600s, recognition of the yakuza as an element of society grew largely during the Tokugawa period. There were two main sources of yakuza: the gamblers (<u>bakuto</u>) and the itinerant merchants (<u>tekiya</u>). The gamblers were also labor bosses who contracted with daimyo for the services of cheap labor and had turned to labor contracting as a means of promoting gambling among the laborers. From the losing numbers (eight-nine-three) in a popular game came the term ya-ku-sa, denoting something no good. The word "yakuza" was later applied to useless, no-good people, including law-breakers.[1] Not all yakuza were gamblers, however.

The word for the itinerant merchants or peddlers, "tekiya," is said to derive from ~ (arrow) and <u>teki</u> (mark) and so designated the sharpies who go after unsuspecting marks.[2] They set up their wares at local markets and festivals and employed numerous tricks to outwit their customers, such as selling less than a full measure of cloth or substituting a used item for one that was sold as new. As in many other Japanese enterprises, the peddlers banded together under a leader who represented their interests.   The tekiya were led by an oyabun who provided them with protection, negotiated with the authorities, allocated space for stalls, and collected rents. The role of the oyabun was recognized by the temple and castle officials who divided territory among the oyabun to avoid potential conflict.[3]

With the advent of the Meiji Restoration, many of the lower class peasants and yakuza gained warrior status by joining the imperial army.   This was a challenge for the samurai as well as an opportunity for these lower-class individuals to improve their status.

For the samurai, the professional warriors ("swords for hire"), the transition from feudalism did not always go smoothly.   The inception of new laws during the Meiji period forced the samurai to give up their way of life, along with their status- defining swords.   Among the nobles, many adapted their lifestyles to agriculture and business.   Others became part of the new governmental bureaucracy.

To a small number of samurai who fell on hard times, the nether world of Japan was enticing. The lure of such yakuza operations as gambling, protection, prostitution, loan sharking, and labor contracting attracted a few former samurai who could use their martial arts skills in these enterprises. From these tainted ties of a century ago, today's yakuza claim their samurai heritage.

In addition to the traditional bakuto and tekiya, in the postwar period strong-arm hoodlums (gurentai or boryokudan) have also been recruited into the yakuza ranks. George De Vos, in his study of fifty families in Tokyo's Arakawa Ward, details the experience of three schoolyard toughs who dominated their middle school and were invited to join a gurentai band. The three young bullies were scouted as possible recruits and then tested by the gurentai.[4] The testing consisted of physical beatings by older thugs to see how much the youngsters could take. Since De Vos' study youth gangs and motorcycle-riding bosozoku have attracted wayward youth. These groups may also have codes of conduct and demand allegiance but there is no connection with the samurai.

The burakumin, Japan's despised untouchable class, faced with the prospect of a lifetime of discrimination, were also attracted to the criminal element. A buraku youth who became a successful yakuza could overcome his outcast background and "pass" in his new world.

Otherwise his prospects were limited to the traditional
<u>burakumin</u> occupations: leather tanning, night soil
removal, or such.[5]

   The form and ritual of the modern yakuza is based
on the moral code once followed by the samurai. Loyalty
to the <u>oyabun</u>, instead of a lord, is foremost.   According
to Lebra, "The relationship between <u>oyabun</u> and <u>kobun</u>
is a copy of the reciprocal obligation between a feudal
lord and vassal. That is why yakuza society, though
illegitimate, is thought to represent the moral values of
traditional Japan."[6]

   The fledgling yakuza's initiation emphasizes
absolute loyalty to one's master. "If necessary, you must
let your wife and children starve and sacrifice your life
on behalf of your <u>oyabun</u>" is an admonishment given
aspiring young recruits. An exchange of sake cups,
presumably in lieu of the ancient ritual of drinking one
another's blood, presages a solemn oath of loyalty. This
loyalty is the ultimate manifestation of <u>giri</u> and <u>ninjo</u>
(human feeling) to the <u>oyabun</u>, and is also extended to
his yakuza brothers.[7]

   The traditional samurai's willingness to sacrifice his
life in battle is just as important for the
criminally-minded yakuza. He must support the house

(ikka) he belongs to in any number of nefarious ways, including extortion, territorial battles, or assassination. He may also be called on to give up his freedom and become a substitute (migawari) for the oyabun by serving a term in jail. To avoid undue police pressure on their subversive group activities, lower ranking yakuza are induced to confess to crimes committed by their elder "brothers" or the gang bosses. This practice allows the police to arrest and jail the supposed criminal while the accomplished mobsters and master boss remain at large.

The migawari experience has become part of the lore of the cult. The yakuza may sacrifice years of his life as a substitute, fulfilling the penal obligation, and dutifully awaiting his reward for spending time in prison. At the end of his imprisonment, the yakuza is met (demukai) at the prison by a welcoming group led by the oyabun and his cohorts, sometimes numbering in the hundreds. A motorcade to the gang's headquarters, or a local restaurant, follows and a ceremonial banquet is held. The yakuza is honored for his service in jail. Other gangs are often in attendance and join in the tribute by presenting monetary gifts. The ex-convict may also be given a promotion within the gang, along with his own "business" to oversee. His position within the group and his future income are thus assured. A long period of incarceration for a heavy crime such as murder is held in higher regard than a lighter sentence for a m1nor infraction. By meeting the yakuza at his release and praising him for his service, the point is clearly made that no amount of punishment can alter the group's kindred spirit and mutual ties.[8]

Another yakuza variation of the samurai code, meant to show the manly traits of endurance and an obliviousness to pain, is elaborate body tattooing. Artful, colored designs picturing fierce battles, samurai, dragons, and serpents are carefully etched with needles into the arms, torso, and buttocks. The completion of a tattoo can take several weeks with the yakuza stoically enduring the agonizing process. The tattoo brazenly shows a firm commitment to his chosen profession, as it marks him for life.

Perhaps best known of the yakuza rituals is finger chopping, a form of self mutilation used to evidence one's sincerity (magokoro). The practice started in the brothels of Edo where women cut off their little fingers and presented them to their lovers as a show of their true love. Yakuza slice off the little finger of the left hand at the first knuckle and present it to their aniki (elder brother), to their oyabun, or to a rival gang to atone for a serious mistake. Further errors can be apologized for by cutting a notch higher to the second knuckle, or clipping the little finger of the right hand.[9] A deep display of magokoro is another reason for this self abuse. Lebra explains simply that "compared with such body communication, verbal repentance would seem to have little persuasive power."[10] Indeed, what could be said that would compare with giving up part of one's body.

The number of yakuza in recognized groups has varied in the postwar period, with the high occurring in 1963 when the National Police Agency listed 184,000 yakuza in 5,216 groups throughout the country. The official figure had dropped to 100,000 in 2,330 groups by 1983,[11] and to about 88,000 by 1991. Authorities attributed the decline to the nation's economic well being. Anti-organized crime laws later reduced the number to about 80,000.

The Yamaguchigumi, which has about 10,000 members, is widely known as a result of the autobiographical history of the group written by former leader Kazuo Taoka (<u>Yamaguchigumi Sandaime: Taoka Kazuo Jiten</u>), which became a best seller. A movie, based on the book and starring Ken Takakura, makes a hero of Taoka.　When a bloody, running battle with the rival Matsudagumi began to spillover and endanger the general public, Taoka--then a notorious celebrity--held a press conference in November 1978, declaring an end to the feud and apologizing to the public and the police for the trouble caused.　The public image of Yamaguchigumi was important to Taoka. Not to be outdone, Matsudagumi boss Tadayoshi Kashi issued a letter to the Osaka police declaring an end to the gang warfare.[12]

Numerous events in the postwar era have kept the yakuza in the limelight. Their association with political figures has been reported often.　Yakuza have violently protested media stories of their activities by smashing newspaper offices, only to have further publicity result. The film industry produced 100 yakuza films a year in the mid-1970s. Popular author Goro Fujita, himself a former yakuza, made a career with over thirty novels romanticizing the virility, bravery, and fatalism of the yakuza.[13]

Junichi Saga's biography of a yakuza-gambler

became a best seller in 1989, again exemplifying the public's strong interest.[14]   Saga, a medical doctor, had recorded the confessions of one of his patients who was suffering from diabetes, which proved fatal. The man's life story included all the elements--a prison sentence as a substitute, finger chopping to apologize for eloping with a woman without the oyabun's permission, his own territory as a gambling boss, bravery, and extreme loyalty.

Yukio Yamanouchi, a former legal advisor to a yakuza group, turned their evil into a pot of gold with a series of gangster novels. Kanashii Hittoman (Lonely Hit Man) hit the movie screens with a rousing success in 1989.   Yamanouchi describes yakuza life as an attractive lure for Japan's burakumin (outcaste people).

Yakuza have assumed a new role in recent years. They frequently serve as enforcers at the shareholders' meetings of giant corporations. These "general meeting experts" (sokaiya) usually function on behalf of management to squelch all dissent and criticism. Their heavy-handed tactics have caused widespread public concern. Yakuza-influenced sokaiya organize using such euphemistic titles as "economic research group," or "study association" to gather company information for blackmail purposes.

Marubeni Iida, the mammoth trading company, suffered public embarrassment during the Lockheed Aircraft bribery scandal in June 1976. Evidence quoted by news reports indicated that Marubeni acted as the major conduit for bribes which went from the aircraft manufacturer to government officials. At a shareholders' meeting a scuffle ensued when yakuza forcefully prevented individual stockholders from asking management potentially damaging questions. The proceedings were televised and broadcast nationwide. Marubeni officials later tried to explain the ruckus away by describing it as a misunderstanding.

Conservative, nationalist elements have attracted yakuza support as paid mercenaries for strike breaking and other labor- management conflicts and for political purposes as bodyguards, for demonstrations, and for use in fund raising. De Vos explains the rightwing's attraction to yakuza as resulting from a need for external authority, which "puts emphasis on the virtues of manliness and bravery in a manner harmonious with a rightist ideology. . . . Hypernationalism goes well with the caricature of the romanticized warrior's code that is used in yakuza groups."[15]

The traditional acceptance of the yakuza's place in society developed from a Robin Hood image of helping the citizenry. In feudal times they were identified as machi yakko (town servants) who protected their villages from pillaging ronin (masterless samurai). Stories about yakuza could also be used to express dissent against official oppression. In this sense, the yakuza became a symbol of resistance to authority.[16] Their valiant, and romanticized, exploits are remembered in many folk tales and songs.

The modern yakuza may show community support by responding rapidly and performing fearlessly as voluntary firefighters.   Or, they may take part in Shinto festivals by snake-dancing through the streets carrying the heavy shrines on their shoulders.[7]   However, just avoiding confrontations with the public at large and participating in limited community activities may not be adequate to allow the yakuza to continue business as usual. Japan's emergence as a leading democratic nation has made the country more conscious of its image abroad and encouraged the public to demand stricter police control of the yakuza. In recent years, a greater number of violent crimes, illegal drug operations, and gun smuggling incidents have caused an increase in public concern over yakuza activity.   Even the yakuza have noted the change.

Shotaro Hayashi, boss of the 200-member Doshidagumi, has complained that the old ways are dying out, values of <u>giri- ninjo</u>, obligation and compassion are fading."[18]   The traditional ethic does not mean as much to the younger, more violent generation.

In an unusual display of public unity, the people of Hamamatsu banded together to confront the local yakuza organization and force the gang to conform to neighborhood standards.   Ichiriki Ikka, a subsidiary of Yamaguchigumi, had built a headquarters building of thick-walled concrete down the street from a primary school. The yakuza painted it black, creating a sinister landmark. The neighbors in the residential area did not want the yakuza so close to the school, or in the area at all. They waged a campaign against the yakuza by restricting all services to the building, including garbage pickup and takeout food deliveries by neighborhood restaurants. The yakuza showed their civilized nature by suing the citizens for the mental anguish they were suffering and in turn were hit with a countersuit. After two years of conflict, including an attempt to assassinate the citizen group's lawyer, the suits were settled out of court in 1988. The yakuza agreed to repaint the building, use the back entrance (away from the school), and restrict their comings and goings. The building was later vacated by the yakuza when a warrant was issued for the arrest of Tetsuya Aono, the yakuza boss who lived there, on weapons charges.

One neighbor summed up the residents' feelings toward the yakuza by saying, "a lot of the older folks around here were a lot more sympathetic with the gang. They remember the old days when Ichiriki Ikka could be helpful. But my generation thinks of drugs and violence when we hear the word 'yakuza'."[19]

Only in recent years has the public started to overcome its innate reticence to become involved. The attitude of acceptance of the yakuza is slowly losing favor as public consciousness changes. Landlords are refusing to rent space to them, neighborhood watch committees limit their activities, police have effected "isolation" campaigns, and even local bathhouses post signs prohibiting tattooed people (a common euphemism for yakuza). However, the same bathhouses may advertise free yakuza movies for their customers, exhibiting both the fear and the fascination felt by the public toward the yakuza.[20]

The heightened vocal public outcry against the criminal element resulted in the anti-yakuza law passed in 1992. The law made it more difficult for yakuza to recruit new members, and also designated the major gangs as illegal criminal organizations.

Nonetheless, the yakuza did show their feelings of oneness with the ordinary citizen by willingly providing food and supplies to victims of the Kobe earthquake in 1995. Although government agencies were criticized for their slow response to the disaster, the yakuza won praise for quickly responding.

While these Robin Hood acts strengthen their claim to a samurai heritage, the distasteful aspects of yakuza crime remain. Their nefarious illegal operations balanced against the concepts of loyalty, duty, and bravery make the organized yakuza groups a unique Japanese enigma. The tumultuous yakuza world, which disregards any purity of purpose, has successfully transformed the admirable traits of the samurai to the underworld of the criminal.

Notes - Chapter 6

1. George A. De Vos with Keiichi Mizushima,
"Organization and Social Function of Japanese Gangs:
Historical Development and Modern Parallels," George
A. De Vos, ed., Socialization for Achievement (Berkeley:
University of California Press, 1973), note, 282.

2. Ibid., note, 283.

3. David Harold Stark, "The Yakuza: Japanese Crime
Incorporated," (Ph.D. diss., University of Michigan,
1981), 30. See Lebra, Japanese Patterns of Behavior,
77-79, for discussion of oyabun-kobun, sensei-deshi, and
sempai-kohai vertical relationships in Japanese society.

4. George A. De Vos and Hiroshi Wagatsuma, Heritage
of Endurance (Berkeley:
University of California Press, 1984), 57.

5. George A. De Vos with Hiroshi Wagatsuma,
"Minority Status and Delinquency in Japan,"
Socialization for Achievement, 389.

6. Lebra, Japanese Patterns, 178.

7.   Ibid., 176.

8.   Stark, 157-159.

9. Donald Kirk, "Crime, Politics and Finger Chopping," New York Times Magazine (12 Dec. 1976), 60.

10. Lebra, Japanese Patterns, 186.

11. David E. Kaplan and Alec Dubro, Yakuza (Reading, Mass.: Addison-Wesley Publishing Co., 1986), 138.

12. "Two Rival Syndicates Declare End to Bloody Gangland War," Japan Times (23 Nov. 1978),2.

13. Ibid., 13.

14. Saga, Junichi. Confessions of a Yakuzu (Tokyo: Kodansha International).

15. De Vos with Mizushima, "Organization and Social Function of Japanese Gangs," Socialization for Achievement, 309.

16. Ibid., 286.

17. Stark, 172.

18. Quoted in Kaplan, 141-143.

19. Quoted in Karl Schoenberger, "Japanese Taking Unprecedented Stand Against Yakuza Menace," Japan Times (14 April 1988), 14.

20. Stark, 139.

Chapter 7

THE FILM INDUSTRY

The samurai spirit weaved its way into the cultural
texture of postwar Japan thanks in large part to the
motion picture industry.   Filmmakers gave movie
audiences reason to glory in and reflect upon the heritage
of the warrior code, presenting both the samurai and his
deviant offspring, the yakuza, in exciting, thrilling
fashion.

After a delayed start, because of SCAP regulations
banning "feudal themes" in movies during the
Occupation period, the industry found a receptive market
for the samurai genre film after censorship rules were
relaxed around 1950. The samurai film emerged to
become a staple, carrying to both movie and television
audiences an exciting message of bravery, loyalty, and a
willingness to die. The genre fulfilled a need for a rebirth
of national pride and respect, instilling traditional
Japanese values in the postwar generation. The
popularity of samurai films encouraged production, and
by 1961-1962 of the 400 films released annually about

40 dealt with samurai. The public's taste eventually changed, and the number of samurai films began to decline. By 1970 only a dozen or so were produced each year and even fewer by 1980.[1]

The decline of samurai films was paralleled, however, by the growing output of yakuza movies. In addition, many jidai geki (period dramas) with non-samurai primary themes have related the samurai spirit, the altered order of status in society, and bushido. Among these have been a number set in the transitional period from the late Tokugawa period to the Meiji Restoration.

The golden years for Japan's film industry were from 1958 to 1964, when an annual average of 1.13 billion people went to the movies (twelve times a year on a per capita basis). Attendance had fallen to 230 million by 1971 (twice a year per capita), and dropped off further to 143 million by 1989 (1.2 times a year per capita, the lowest rate among the world's developed countries). The number of movie theaters grew from 1,600 just after the war to 6,000 in 1957 and then dropped off steadily thereafter, reaching 1,900 in 1989.[2]

During the golden years, theaters presented a new double feature each week, pushing producers to churn out a world record of 600 pictures in 1956. Quality was less of a concern than quantity.3

The advent of television was a major factor in the decline of the motion picture industry. Films were aired on TV three years after release, with approximately forty movies per week available on home screens.[4] Widespread exposure to bushido was facilitated by television. The postwar generation was bombarded with a proliferation of jidai geki and chambara (swordfighting) made-for-television movies.

The tremendous latent interest in the exploits of samurai came to the attention of filmmakers during the recovery period after the war. The disheartening failure of the war effort had left the public thirsting for heroes. However, for several years SCAP prohibited films with revenge in their plots, antidemocratic themes, or swordfighting scenes, making the production of samurai films difficult at best.[5] Even the perennial favorite Chushingura was not allowed, because it affirmed the loyalty of the forty-seven samurai to their lord and highlighted their eventual revenge.[6] Not until 1949 were regulations relaxed.

From that point on the film industry attacked the market with samurai films. "The resurrection of period drama after the Occupation was probably not so much a restoration of feudal thought," one authority suggested, "as a continuation of the old fear--namely, that postwar Japan's weakness would continue unless the will and pride of the samurai was preserved."[7]

Joan Mellen, in her study of Japanese films, notes that Japanese directors used the Restoration and the Pacific War in their films to try to answer three questions plaguing the nation: what does it mean to be a Japanese; what identity shall Japan and the Japanese assume; and what is unique about Japan and how can it be preserved? [8]

The search for the meanlng of "Japan," a spiritual definition of the country, was a theme in many major Japanese films.[9] In <u>Chikamatsu Monogatari</u> (A Story from Chikamatsu), director Kenji Mizoguchi contrasted the growing wealth and power of the merchant class with the position of the poor, but noble samurai. The decadent merchant abused his power to the detriment of his employees, while at the same time assuming the airs of a samurai. The film showed the continuing prevalence of feudal relationships in the emerging capitalist world.[10]

Director Akira Kurosawa's <u>Rashomon</u>, starring Toshiro Mifune and produced in 1950, gave the postwar film industry a respectable standing by gaining international acclaim. It won the 1951 Venice Festival Grand Prize and the 1952 Academy Award for Best Foreign Film. Rashomon told the story of a weak samurai who failed to live up to the bushido code and was killed. The nature of man, as reflected in the code, was tied to the actions and interpretations of four central characters.[11]

Seven Samurai, a Kurosawa work of 1954, also starred Mifune. It was a forceful account of a poor village saved from marauders by a good hearted group of wandering samurai. The tragic plight of the peasants--emphasized by the stark black-and-white imagery of the film--called for all the strength and warrior skills of their valiant saviors. The film highlighted the positive aspects of the samurai, but also showed the respect and even fear with which the villagers treated them. The final battle against the horde of ravaging bandits gave moviegoers the anticipated swordplay and showed heroism against tremendous odds. The scene was almost anti-climactic. The victory of the samurai--the forces of Good conquering Evil--was a foregone conclusion. This simple, if fanciful, story became a classic in the film industry, copied in the West by John Sturges's production The Magnificent Seven, starring Yul Brynner. David Desser has commented that Seven Samurai "virtually created the serious contemporary samurai film."[12]

The Toho trilogy <u>Samurai</u> (1954-1955), directed by Hiroshi Inagaki, became another major production of the times. Great battles, duels of honor, and unrequited love all found the place in this epic which traced the life and adventures of the man considered Japan's greatest swordsman, Musashi Miyamoto.[13]   Mifune, in the lead role, went from a brash upstart in Part I, <u>Samurai</u>, to an accomplished warrior knowledgeable in the ways of bushido by the end of Part III, <u>Musashi and Kojiro</u>. Director Inagaki's presentation of the renowned hero of the past created an idealized, symbolic version of everything the samurai stood for .[14]

What effect did period dramas such as these have on the viewing public? Donald Richie, the dean of Western critics of Japanese films, observed that

> despite the surface modernity of the country, the past continues to live. A part of the Japaneseness of the Japanese is this unquestioning and even casual acceptance of the past as a definite part of the contemporary life. . . .   In a film as late, and as commercial as <u>Musashi Miyamoto</u>, shown abroad as <u>Samurai</u>, one can still feel the strength of the

original concept: Musashi is not a mindless clotheshorse; he is a modern man.[15]

Realistic historical films are commonly accepted, Richie notes, with "an agreement from the man in the balcony that his problems were much like those of the samurai on the screen."[16]

The Shin Toho company recorded a major financial success in 1956 with its production of <u>Emperor Meiji and the Great Russo- Japanese War</u>. Shin Toho's president Mitsugu Okura announced that the film was being made to revive the spirit of patriotism in the hearts of the public. The film, directed by Kunio Watanabe, known for ultranationalistic pictures, emphasized the so-called "imperial way." It was the first movie to portray a Japanese emperor on the screen. Moviegoers thronged to see it. <u>Emperor Meiji</u> grossed five times its costs of 80 million yen.[17]

The image of the <u>ronin</u> (masterless samurai) attached itself to Mifune with his starring roles in Kurosawa's highly regarded <u>Yojimbo</u> and its sequel, <u>Sanjuro</u>.   The transitional early Tokugawa period, when samurai were reduced to acting as bodyguards for the merchant class, serves as the background in a dog-eat-dog (or man) world. The message is graphically--and gruesomely-- portrayed in an early sequence showing a dog trotting by with a human hand in its mouth. "The hungry dogs," masterless samurai and outlaws in the film, were attracted by the smell of blood.[18]

In Japan, as anywhere else, the viewing public makes its own choice in effect determining through ticket sales what films will be produced. The industry first tests the market with experimental or low budget films, then goes into full production on anything that looks like a box office winner. Although the industry's advertising molds popular opinion to view and approve what it produces, public taste cannot be manipulated beyond where it is already prepared to go. The public wanted heroes, so the motion picture producers created the bravest, most spirited--and often most handicapped--samurai heroes of all time. Because they were first and foremost part of the entertainment business, samurai films were based less on fact than fiction.

The existence of the samurai code was an important tenet of the jidai geki. Producers rightfully assumed that the audience was aware of the guiding principles of bushido, but not the shades of interpretation that might occur.   Since the rules of warrior life were fixed, changes in plots were often related to misplaced loyalties or prior duties and obligations which outweighed current relationships. The films dramatized again and again the theme of giri-ninjo. The handicapped samurai, such as the successful series on blind Zato Ichi, provided an added twist. The lead samurai usually displayed all the traits worthy of manliness, becoming the tateyaku (macho main actor), as compared to a nimaime (handsome, effete type).   The tateyaku fought for glory and honor, while the nimaime found romance. Young male moviegoers preferred the tateyaku, while female TV viewers favored the nimaime.[19]

With contrived plots, technical innovations, short swords used for self-destruction, and long swords splashing enemy blood across the screen, the heritage of the samurai was consciously mythicized.   Desser cites two conditions needed to successfully turn historical fact into cinematic mythology, and in postwar Japan both were there: the industrial capability to mass produce films, and the ability of the society to support their continued production.[20]

With the free enterprise system in effect in the 1950s, the samurai film, which had been popular before the war, reasserted itself. "The new Japan now needed to redefine, remythicize its image to make the past correspond to the present," Desser observed. The samurai film became the vehicle with which to do it.[21]

Characteristic of Japanese films is the practice of remaking plays or movies that have been successful in the past, using currently popular actors. Another popular approach is adapting old favorites to modern life. Chushingura has been redone many times. Its wartime version stressed the blind loyalty of soldiers offering their lives for the emperor and the country. When NHK redid it as a television production in 1964, and again in 1975, the loyal retainers became fighters for "demokurashi" against the feudal and oppressive Tokugawa regime. Another version of the play appeared in the film Salaryman Chushingura, with the office politics and corruption of a trading company as the background. The ultimate and frolicsome adaptation, aimed at a younger audience, cavorted across the screen as the animated cartoon Wan Wan Chushingura, featuring a cast of dogs. The common factor of giri tied all these productions together, with retainers in their

various forms exhibiting loyalty to their leader.[22]   A
Tokyo temple which claims the graves of the
Chushingura samurai attracts thousands each year on the
anniversary of mass suicide.

What has been referred to as the "super
samurai" was best exemplified in the Zato Ichi series,
starring Shintaro Katsu as a blind, rough-and-tumble
masseur-swordfighter who conquers wrongdoers
everywhere. Close up, telescoped views of his ear
listening to an opponent's movements emphasized the
sense of hearing.   Zato Ichi could easily detect the
sound of a sword slicing toward him through the air, and
nimbly make an effective countermeasure. The series
first appeared in 1962, starting a parade of 25 film
adventures in which evil-doers were punished and the
good were rewarded.   The series outlived its original
producers, Daiei, which collapsed in red ink, and moved
to Toho in 1971.   Zato Ichi himself, star actor Shintaro
Katsu, produced and directed the last one in 1973, which
was to die a box office death. Thereafter, the series came
back to life again on television.[23]

What could be better than a successful series, such
as Zato Ichi, and a successful serious samurai epic, such
as Yojimbo?   The answer was to have the stars of each

combining their talents in one joint production.   The movie world's attempt to cash in by casting the two together was a contrived compost called <u>Zato Ichi Meets Yojimbo</u> (1970).   The inevitable duel between Katsu and Mifune ended with a frustrating non-climax, leaving only producers at Daiei breathless and mortally wounded.[24]   Years later Zato Ichi's powers failed Katsu again--this time in the mundane world--when he was arrested on drug charges.

From samurai defense of helpless villagers and wealthy merchants it took only a short step to tall tales of chivalrous yakuza defending against samurai excesses. In place of bushido, the yakuza became champions of <u>ninkyodo</u> (chivalrous code), while still practicing loyalty, bravery, and a willingness to die. Yakuza emerged as noble outlaws, fighting against the corrupt modern age.[25]

The new film genre contained a standard list of scenes: the special yakuza introduction to a gang boss; the establishment of a <u>giri</u> relationship; a kidnapping, assassination or double cross; a gambling scene with colorful body tattoos on display; self- inflicted finger chopping; the gang welcome after a prison release; and, finally, a gallant death in a sword or gun battle which resolves the <u>giri-ninjo</u> problem.   Illegal activities, including extortion, gambling, or smuggling became the vehicle to show human relationships, such as the yakuza "family" ties.   Although Mellen labels them "hack-formula, potboilers all," generally containing little of cinematic value, she also sees them as proposing "a return to the values of the past, particularly to those of the samurai culture."[26]

The Jirocho series, produced by Toei from 1962 to 1964, provided the forerunners for the copies to follow. Based on the adventures of Shimizu no Jirocho, a legendary gambler-yakuza- Robin Hood, Jirocho bridged the gap from jidai geki to yakuza as a genre.[27]   The series also marked its star, Koji Tsuruta, as the king of yakuza actors.

Indeed, if Mifune and Katsu were the premier samurai, then Tsuruta and Ken Takakura led the yakuza pack.   Takakura, who achieved virtual cult status for his gangster-hero portrayals, became one of the Orient's top stars, revered by both student radicals and the political far right.[28]

After the big box office draw of The Godfather in Japan, yakuza documentaries were produced, including Yamaguchigumi Sandaime, the story of Yamaguchigumi boss Kazuo Taoka, and Shura no Mure, based on the life of Kakuji Inagawa, leader of the Inagawagumi. Plots based on tales of the major gangster organizations begat more of the same. Other variations included actress Junko Fujii as a female yakuza, replete with a cross-the-back tattoo, and an American entry into the field, a co-production starring Ken Takakura and Robert Mitchum, titled simply The Yakuza. In an amazing acceptance of the yakuza creed, perennial tough guy Mitchum chops off his little finger to show his sincerity to Takakura.

In the make believe world of the movies, the yakuza attempted to replace the samurai, giving the Japanese something related to their belief in bushido. As Paul Schrader puts it, "Sacrificial death is a badge of honor, a small price to pay should it succeed in resurrecting the code of bushido. The very fact that yakuza films can draw upon widely felt feudal responses in the audience is a measure of the extent to which bushido still lives in the culture."29   If films reveal something deep and essential about a culture, then the samurai values were still there in the Japanese idea.

Audiences did respond for several years. Toei, the leader in yakuza films, made from 26 to 30 between 1968 and 1972, the peak years.[30]   But whatever socially redeeming value they may have had, as tastes changed, commercially the samurai and the yakuza gave way. The film industry's golden period faded in the 1970s, leading Richie to ask rhetorically, "how is it that one of the world's most honest and aesthetically advanced cinemas became the undistinguished, pandering, money-grubbing industry we find in Japan today? "[31]

Since Richie posed that question in 1983 the industry has improved its stature with such films as director Shohei Imamura's Kuroi Arne (Black Rain), which earned great praise from Richie upon its release in 1988,[32] Tampopo, a mod, mad, and funny version of a spaghetti-western, and Heaven and Earth, a samurai epic so big it was filmed in the Canadian Rockies to accommodate the 800 horses and 3,000 extras used in the battle scenes.

But regardless of what has happened to Japan's film industry, the samurai spirit continues to be depicted in the popular media and to find a ready audience in the Japanese public. Television continues to keep the spirit alive with daily offerings of samurai soap operas. The Tokyo Broadcasting System's series Mito Komon, a formula drama about an incognito traveling samurai, has aired over six hundred episodes since its start in 1969. It averaged a high audience rating of 29 percent, making

it the leader among TV's samurai offerings. Why do
people watch <u>Mito Komon</u> and other samurai pot boilers
on TV? The answer, according to an official at TV
Asahi, is that people can relieve the stress and tension of
their everyday lives by watching arrogant officials and
greedy merchants meet their doom. The contrived but
happy endings please the audience.[33] The message
repeated over and over again is that the samurai who acts
in accordance with the code will win over the forces of
evil, a simple answer to everyday problems.

The code has been tarnished by its daily exposure
to the video's electric glow, its once strong beam of
purity dulled by overuse and commercialism.
Nonetheless, the samurai spirit carries on as a powerful,
forceful part of the nation's culture.

Notes - Chapter 7

1. David Desser, "Toward a Structural Analysis of the Postwar Samurai Film," Quarterly Review of Film Studies, 8 (1983), 25.

2. "Films: Phoenix or Flop?" Japan Quarterly, 19 (1972), 129; International Motion Picture Almanac, ed. Barry Monush (New York: Quigley Publishing Co., 1991), 698.

3. Akira Iwasaki, "The Battle of the Screens," Japan Quarterly, 4 (1957),442.

4. International Film Guide, ed. Peter Cowie (London: The Tantivy Press, 1978), 217.

5. Tadao Sato, Currents in Japanese Cinema, trans. Gregory Barrett (Tokyo: Kodansha International Ltd., 1982), 255.

6. Ibid., 44.

7. Ibid., 26.

8. Joan Mellen, The Waves at Genii's Door (New York: Pantheon Books, 1976), 9.

9. Ibid.

10. Ibid., 17-19.

11. Keiko I. McDonald, Cinema East (East Brunswick, N.J.: Associated University Presses, 1983), 23.

12. David Desser, <u>The Samurai Films of Akira Kurosawa</u> (Ann Arbor, MI: UMI Research Press, 1983), 6.

13. Beverly Bare Buehrer, <u>Japanese Films</u> (Jefferson, North Carolina: McFarland & Co., 1990), 103.

14. Ibid., 106.

15. Donald Richie, <u>Japanese Cinema</u> (Garden City, New York: Doubleday & Co., 1971), 43, 45.

16. Ibid., 48.

17. Akira Iwasaki, "The Battle of the Screens," <u>Japan Quarterly</u>, 4 (1957), 444.

18. Keiko I. McDonald, "Swordsmanship and Gamesmanship: Historical Kurosawa's Milieu in Yojimbo," <u>Literature/Film Quarterly</u>, 8 (1980), 188-190.

19. Sato, 37. 20. Desser, <u>Samurai Films of Kurosawa</u>, 18.

21. Ibid., 22.

22. Ian Buruma, <u>A Japanese Mirror</u> (London: Jonathon Cape Ltd., 1984), 157.

23. Buehrer, 217.

24. Ibid., 212-215.

25. Buruma, 170.

26. Mellen, 121-122.

27. Paul Schrader, "Yakuza-Eiga, A Primer," <u>Film Comment</u> (Jan. 1974), 10.

28. Ibid., 15.

29. Mellen, 123.

30. Schrader, 10.

31. Donald Richie, "The State of the Japanese Film," <u>Japan Quarterly</u>, 30 (1983), 176.

32. Frank Segers, "Japanese Bet on New Pic 'Black Rain, and So Do Experts," <u>Variety</u> (3 - 9 May 1989), 409.

33. Yuko Naito, "Familiarity Breeds Content in Samurai Dramas," <u>Japan Times</u>, weekly international edition (8-14 April 1991), 13.

Chapter 8

THE BUSINESSMEN

When the fire and the fury of World War II were extinguished, the next formidable task that Japan faced was the reconstruction of the devastated country. The "miraculous" recovery of the Japanese economy, starting from 1945, encompassed a series of well documented economic factors--and an underlying cultural reason also, the samurai spirit of the nation's business leaders.

With postwar conditions similar to those of the post-Restoration period, the new democracy imposed upon Japan by the Allies spurred business development. The samurai of the Meiji period had been inspired by a basic doctrine: "what's good for business is good for the nation," and in 1945 that was true again. Despite the economic purge enacted by the Supreme Commander of Allied Powers (SCAP), many of the prewar industrial leaders reappeared, along with a new crop of entrepreneurs. Both the prewar "old boys" and the postwar generation were imbued with a dedication to aiding their nation's recovery.

The samurai business spirit first appeared in the Meiji era when, after two hundred and fifty years of Tokugawa isolationist policy, Japan was forced to open its doors to the West and acknowledge the technological gap it faced. The need to learn Western ways, to acquire scientific knowledge, and to introduce modern banking, cotton spinning, railways, large-scale shipbuilding, mining, and other industries was urgent. The samurai, stripped of their special status, were encouraged to take up business to benefit Japan in its struggle to catch up with the advanced know-how of the West. As a class, the samurai were educated, disciplined, and achievement oriented. For these elite warriors, engaging in business became a patriotic duty to save the nation, no longer an unsavory practice engaged in by lowly merchants seeking profit. The government was concerned that if Japan failed to strengthen itself adequately, it would become an economic colony for Europe and the United States-- or lose its independence altogether.

Through the teachings of such men as Eiichi Shibusawa (1840- 1931), considered the father of modern Japanese enterprise, and Yukichi Fukuzawa, the Western-thinking educator, samurai were encouraged to venture forward as businessmen. Both Shibusawa and Fukuzawa had been part of government missions to Europe and America in the 1860s and were impressed by the advanced civilizations they saw there.

Although samurai followed the code of bushido, Shibusawa interpreted the code as encompassing justice, integrity, chivalry, magnanimity, and courtesy. The business ethic that he advocated included five requisites: education, honesty, virtue, personality, and the building of modern enterprise combining Confucian principles and the abacus.

In his thinking, the bushido contained valid business precepts and could be proclaimed as the "Way of the New Merchant." Service for the public good in business practice was urged as part of the new samurai responsibilities. To assist entrepreneurs, in 1871 the Ministry of Finance published two explanatory books, Rikkai Ryakusoku (Outline of Setting Up Companies) written by Shibusawa, and Kaisha Ben (On Companies), a translation of a chapter on banking taken from a Western economics text.[1]

While the West was superior in technology, the Japanese relied on the determination and virtue found in the samurai spirit. The new era of civilization and enlightenment (bummei kaika) became associated with samurai status and officialdom. The first Economic White Book, issued in 1884, listed the requirements for building Japanese industries. Three factors were cited and relative weights assigned to them: the spirit, five parts; laws and regulations, four parts; and capital, one part.[2] The Meiji government promoted progressiveness and the welfare of the nation by adopting Western methods for use by their "spirited" people.

Of all industries, banking was considered "modern," a service to the nation, and enticing to many samurai, who could invest the bonds issued to them for their commuted pensions as share capital in new banks. Banking allowed samurai to become leaders in the field by reading Shibusawa's treatise on the subject, learning the system, and following the banking regulations. By 1893, 193 national banks had been chartered with 76 percent of the capital supplied by former nobility and samurai. As a result the national banks were sometimes called "samurai banks." Many others founded private banks, which soon outnumbered the national banks.[3]

In contrast, the merchant class was slow to change from the concept of a bank as a money exchange and personal loan business to that of a bank as a community-centered organization dealing in investment capital. The merchants followed traditional practices as money lenders. In other business operations too, the merchants adhered to their code which required loyalty, obedience, and unrestricted service to the merchant house, with obedience put above profit making. The House of Mitsui traces its banking operations, in traditional form, to 1683, but only the possible loss of lucrative government business convinced the Houses of Mitsui and Ono to form a bank as a joint stock company. Shibusawa became president of the bank.[4]

The educated samurai also saw the advantages of adopting the newly introduced form of business enterprise, the joint stock company, a form that Shibusawa championed. Through a corporate structure the needed capital for major projects could be gathered, management expertise hired, and shareholders satisfied. However, the merchants clung to the traditional concept of the merchant house as a family organization.

The idea of service to the nation was evident in a petition to the government in 1873 requesting permission to construct a railway from Tokyo to Aomori. The nobles making the petition reflected the thinking of the times by saying:

> Although we are recipients of an <u>on</u> from the Imperial House as large as the ocean and as high as the mountains, we have become inactive people without purpose, not able to do anything for the country. This makes us ashamed of ourselves. Recently some members of the nobility, returning from England, told us the story of the railways. Hence, we resolved to start a railway company ourselves and thus contribute at least a small part toward the development of our country.[5]

Shibusawa, who turned to private business after serving as head of the government's Taxation Bureau, sponsored a technical student, Takeo Yamabe, sent to England in 1878 to make a special study of cotton spinning In Manchester. Until then, Japan's spinning industry showed small profits, was subsidized by the government, and lacked the funds and expertise to expand. Mill size was only 2,000 spindles or less. Upon his return, Yamabe directed the construction of the largest mill in the country with 10,500 spindles using steam power. Shibusawa secured the capital for this large undertaking, which began operation as the Osaka Spinning Mill in 1883. A year later, the mill paid dividends of 18 percent. The company added another mill of 20,800 spindles in 1886 to become one of the largest industries in Japan and the first to prove successful in competition with the West. Much of the labor for these new mills carne from former samurai-class women,[6] and the daughters of poverty stricken, landless farmers.

Shibusawa provided his expertise as director, organizer, and advisor to some 500 organizations, including government agencies, public organizations, and private enterprise. In short he became the elder statesman of Japanese business. Throughout his life he advocated modern business methods conducted with traditional values and ethics.[7]

Fukuzawa founded a school of western learning, Keio Gijuku (today's Keio University), which became a prlme source for government and major company recruits. Most of Fukuzawa's students were samurai offspring.   Fukuzawa translated foreign books, compiled a Japanese-English dictionary, and was a leader of the intellectual movement championing the cause of universal equality under the law. He wrote extensively on the equality of man under the democratic principles espoused during the Meiji period.

"Heaven did not create any man above man nor any man below man," he wrote.

To the rural peasants, farmers, tenants, tradesmen, or small village merchants the theoretical teachings of Shibusawa and Fukuzawa made little difference. Ideals of equality were slow to reach the common people. They continued to follow traditional class patterns of loyalty, hard work, and submission to group discipline. Even after the turn of the century it was most difficult for a student from a tenant or worker's family to get to college. The sons of former samurai still predominated, with the top graduates becoming government officials and major company executives.

To say that a samurai spirit was the primary motivational factor of entrepreneurs in the Meiji period would be overemphasizing its importance. Indeed, in his study of the Mitsubishi zaibatsu, Yamamura argues that existing technology and business techniques may have been more important than Confucian ethics and the samurai spirit.[8] Nonetheless, historians consistently noted the presence of Confucian ethics, samurai values, and other undefined characteristics termed the Japanese spirit (yamato damashii). Likewise, the government emphasized this attitude to its people for decades to come. In the series of international confrontations leading to World War II, the unique Japanese spirit was recognized as a major strength of the nation.

Another major factor were the zaibatsu (financial cliques). Led by Mitsui, Mitsubishi, Sumitomo, and Yasuda they began to flourish during the Meiji period, encouraged by the government to enter new industries and aided with substantial subsidies. Mitsui's origins are traced to a merchant family, while Mitsubishi was founded by Yataro Iwasaki, a farmer's son who bought a lowly samurai title.[9] The zaibatsu were unique in that control was maintained through familial relationships, arranged marriages, interlocking directorships, holding companies, and their own commercial banks. Their growth mirrors the expansion of Japanese industry through the Meiji, Taisho, and Showa periods to World War II.

Zaibatsu trading companies established offices overseas providing Japan's growing industries with markets for manufactured exports and sources for imports of raw materials. The zaibatsu also took advantage of military conquests in Korea, China, and Manchuria to promote profit-making opportunities in those countries. The nefarious Greater East Asia Co-Prosperity Sphere was associated with the continental expansion of the zaibatsu.

The financial strength of the zaibatsu grew to such an extent that by 1944, the four main zaibatsu banks made 74.9 percent of all Japan's bank loans. Their grip on the national economy was pervasive: Mitsui controlled 46 subsidiaries and 143 affiliated companies; Mitsubishi controlled 28 subsidiaries and 153 affiliates; Sumitomo 19 subsidiaries and 186 affiliates, and Yasuda 19 subsidiaries and 18 affiliates.[10]

At the end of World War II the Allies were determined to thoroughly dismantle the structure which had built Japan's war machine, including the zaibatsu. There was no question that vanquished lands overseas would be returned, military materiel confiscated, war criminals tried, and political leaders of the Japanese war effort purged--all factors that a defeated nation could expect. But the purge went further than that and included the economic sector as well. For the business world this meant the dissolution of the zaibatsu and the splitting up of companies dominant in their industries. The intent of SCAP's original plan to dismantle the economic foundation of the war machine was soon altered. The policy shifted from reform to recovery. The ultimate aim carne to be establishing business according to democratic principles that would avoid great accumulations of wealth and power, while removing from the scene those persons who might impede the democratization process.[11]

The zaibatsu were targeted for supporting the military machine and promoting the Greater East Asia Co-Prosperity Sphere for their own profit. General Douglas MacArthur termed their record one of economic oppression and exploitation at home, aggression and spoilage abroad. "It was these very persons," he said, "born and bred as feudalistic overlords, who held the lives and destiny of the majority of Japan's people in virtual slavery, and who, working in closest affiliation with the military, geared the country with both the tools and the will to wage aggressive war. . . . These are the persons who, under the purge, are to be removed from influencing the course of Japan's future economy." President Harry S. Truman was advised by the State Department that the zaibatsu and the military were mutually dependent. [12]

The result was a Joint Chiefs of Staff directive to MacArthur stating:

> You will require the Japanese to establish a public agency responsible for reorganizing Japanese business in accordance with the military and economic objectives of your [command]. You will require this agency to submit, for approval by you, plans for dissolving large Japanese industrial and banking combines or other large concentrations of business control. [13]

In the plans the Japanese were to submit, persons who were active proponents of militant nationalism and aggression were prohibited from retaining "positions of important responsibility or influence." Criteria for judging economic leaders included participation in the war effort, but a willingness to work toward peaceful ends was a favorable mitigating factor. Aside from the zaibatsu, which following pressure from SCAP formulated their own plans for dissolution, the economic purge was not nearly as far reaching as the goal. According to the Potsdam Declaration, "There must be eliminated for all time the authority and influence of those who have deceived and misled the people of Japan." Of the 210,000 people eventually purged, only 1,898 were in the so-called business elite category, most of those purged (167,000) came from the military. Many of the economic purges were appealed, and the number actually effected was reduced. The Japanese ended the purge in its entirety the day after the Peace Treaty became official in 1952. The eternity of "for all time" had ended in only a few years .[14]

Obviously, the military represented the greatest threat to the peace of the world, and accordingly received the most attention from SCAP.   In turn, SCAP's emphasis on the military allowed Japan's postwar leaders to place the burden of responsibility for the war on the military machine. The people, they said, were misled.

In October, 1947, Joseph B. Keenan, the chief prosecutor for the war crimes trials, cleared the business world of guilt by stating, "We have neither been offered nor have we found evidence of instances where prominent business and industrial leaders conspired with anyone to plan or initiate the war . . . It's quite different from Germany.

There the industrialists held the stirrups while Hitler mounted the beast.   If the bankers and commercial leaders here held the stirrups it was at the point of a gun."[15]

For the business people facing chaotic conditions in the autumn of 1945, the disastrous end to the war brought about a strange new beginning, one complete with foreign forces on their soil. There was no choice for the defeated nation but to recognize the strength and authority of the Allied Powers and to turn to the rebuilding process. Indeed, the only course was to adopt the democracy and policies implemented by SCAP.   A new beginning would be made, and the business community would work to revitalize its homeland, much in the manner of the Meiji era samurai who patriotically endeavored to protect their country. The fear of becoming a colonized nation of the third world that the Restoration leaders had faced almost a hundred years ago was present again.   Businessmen reacted with determination to rebuild Japan's economy and reestablish her place among the leading industrial nations of the world.

Given the prewar leadership positions of the zaibatsu companies, it was not surprising that these firms, with new, younger middle-management executives moving up as directors, once again moved to the forefront of industry.   It did not take long to reestablish the familiar oyagaisha-kogaisha (parent company- subsidiary company) status.   Employees of Mitsubishi Shoji, which was broken up in 1947, started over and gradually merged with other trading companies. In 1954 a new Mitsubishi Shoji was formed, which then became the nation's largest trading company.

Just as in the past, small businesses became the subcontractors and suppliers for the giants and depended on them for their livelihood. Although the SCAP reforms dissected the maze of formal interlocking arrangements and financial shareholdings of the zaibatsu, the personal loyalties and obligations linking management personnel and their underlings could not be abrogated. The bonds that held these relationships were tied to tradition, too tangled for mere directives to unravel. There were two types of business leaders who emerged in the postwar period: those who were with established companies which resumed by turning from war production to peaceful competition, and the new entrepreneurs who struggled to create a niche for themselves in the business world. Both types were products of the prewar educational system, including the moral and military training which had its origins In the Meiji era reforms.

Among the established prewar executives who overcame the travail and turbulence of the postwar years none exemplified the samurai spirit better than Matsutaro Shoriki. His background, interests, and past career tied Shoriki to the code of bushido.[16]

Shoriki was born in 1885 in Toyama, on the Sea of Japan, to a family of three sons and seven daughters. His father built earthworks and bridges in the area and was granted the privilege of wearing a sword. As a youth Shoriki was physically weak and encouraged to play outdoors to build his bodily strength. He showed early promise as a student, doing well in primary school, but tapered off to place near the bottom of his graduating class in middle school. He took up the martial art of kendo, becoming adept and spirited in his fighting. During his high school days in Kanazawa, Shoriki shined as a member of the judo team, using floor technique as his specialty. In what he later described as "the greatest day of my life," Shoriki fought for his school against the team captain of a Kyoto high school who was graded higher than he was. Shoriki used a surprise attack, which he likened to the Okehazama battle of Nobunaga Oda, to floor his opponent and secure an upset victory.

While doing well physically, scholastically he continued to struggle, although he was able to enter the University of Tokyo. His record there was considered mediocre, and he was unable to pass the civil service examination until a year after graduation.

Shoriki entered the police department as an inspector and soon showed exemplary skill under pressure and an ability to take control and defuse tense, potentially violent situations. He assisted in quelling the rice riots in 1918 and the demonstrations for manhood

suffrage in 1920. He was also involved in the crackdown
on the early communist movement, marking him as a
lifelong enemy of the communists. As a police inspector,
he attracted attention for his common sense,
understanding, and strength of character at a time when
brute force was the commonly used police tactic.
Shoriki was also credited for assuming proper
responsibility for the acts of those under his command.

By 1923, with 13 years of experlence, Shoriki had
become chief of the Criminal Affairs Bureau.   On
December 27 a lone terrorist, attempting to assassinate
the Crown Prince (later to become Emperor Hirohito),
fired a shot which broke the glass of the prince's car. The
Crown Prince was unharmed and the terrorist
immediately arrested, however the responsibility for
such an outrageous act could not escape the government.
The Cabinet members offered their resignations, which
were refused, but the duty of the police to avoid such
incidents was considered within Shoriki's control.
Although not personally involved, he received an
immediate dismissal, becoming the scapegoat of the
affair.   Only a month later, in January 1924, on the
occasion of the Crown Prince's marriage, an amnesty
was granted to political offenders, and Shoriki was
officially forgiven.   He then had the opportunity to
return to police service without penalty, continuing a
promising career.   However, he decided to try his hand

in private business instead.

During his tenure with the police, Shoriki had become friends with many leading politicians and businessmen. Through those contacts he was introduced to an opportunity in the newspaper field, although he knew nothing of running a newspaper at that time. Former Home Minister Shimpei Goto offered his assistance and provided Shoriki with financial backing to purchase the Yomiuri Shimbun, a minor newspaper in financial trouble and with a circulation of only 40,000 at the time.

Shoriki brought great energy to the Yomiuri when he took it over in 1924, instilling a new attitude of hard work and financial integrity. He eliminated wasteful practices, excessive overtime, and advertising kickbacks, enforced subscription collections, and started a series of editorial improvements that would change Japanese newspapers forever. Under his leadership the Yomiuri became promotion minded, appealing to the interests of Tokyo's common people. The paper added special columns and features on a variety of subjects, including household hints, radio programs, fishing tips, mah-jongg, and horse race handicapping. It promoted national championship go matches, offered subscribers free sightseeing tours to the volcanic island of Oshima, and was first to introduce comic cartoons. Shoriki was receptive to new ideas and offbeat news-making stories.

He sent a reporter-photographer team to Mt. Mihara, an active volcano on Oshima well known as a "lover's leap" for despondent young lovers. The team made a descent of 1,250 feet into the crater. Their reports described for Yomiuri readers a hellish scene of sulfuric fumes, lava, jagged crags, and the remains of a recent suicide twisted among the rocks.

The public liked what the Yomiuri was doing and responded well. Circulation rose over the years to 123,000 in 1927, 220,000 in 1930, and 500,000 in 1933.

Shoriki's greatest promotion still continues today with Yomiuri sponsorship. As his own sports background was in budo (martial arts), he knew little of baseball, but he was convinced by his staff to invite an American all-star team to Japan in 1931. The barnstorming tour was highly successful, the team playing seventeen games in nine cities. This was followed by an even greater undertaking in 1934 when the famous Babe Ruth came to Japan. Ruth and his team were greeted with a parade along the Ginza with a crowd estimated at one million people. The Americans played to overflow crowds everywhere. The impact of baseball's popularity was not lost on Shoriki. He formed the Yomiuri Giants baseball team and sent it to the United States in 1935 for an exhibition tour, with all the games duly reported in the newspaper. Shoriki's support led to the formation of the Japanese professional leagues with teams sponsored by major corporations.

On the editorial front, the Yomiuri added an afternoon edition in November 1931 to provide readers with late news of Manchurian events. Yomiuri finally became competitive with the well established Asahi and Mainichi, which already had afternoon editions. Overseas coverage was extended by sending news correspondents abroad and also by contracting with an American news agency, International News Service.

Circulation grew to 880,000 by 1937, making Yomiuri the largest paper in Tokyo. In 1942, when the government needed an accurate audit on which to base newsprint rationing, Yomiuri's combined morning and evening circulation was 1,560,000.

As the publisher of a major newspaper, Shoriki lent his name to numerous political and social organizations, including the Martial Virtues Association, founded in 1895 to promote the samurai spirit among the nation's youth, and the Imperial Rule Assistance Association (IRAA), organized in 1940 to support the emperor and to promote national unity. The aims of the IRAA were to strengthen national defense, to inculcate the way of "faithful loyal subjects," to "exalt the great Divine Way," and to serve as a medium for transmitting the wishes of the government to the people. Clearly Shoriki was in a key position to influence Japanese public opinion in the prewar years. When the war ended, he easily fit the category of people to be purged for having been in a "position of authority and influence" in the media, which had advocated aggression and militant nationalism. Shoriki was also purged because he was a leading member of such ultranationalistic organizations as the IRAA.

Shoriki accepted the purge fatalistically. He was a member of the class that would pay the price for his nation's folly. But two postwar events occurred which were to test his character more severely: the strike at Yomiuri and his imprisonment as a suspected war criminal.

With the war's end, leading executives and editors at the Asahi and Mainichi resigned in response to demands by organized editorial writers and staffers that they take responsibility for supporting the military. At Yomiuri, Shoriki stood firm against some 40 staffers who demanded his resignation. He said the responsibility was for everyone to share. He refused to resign. Instead, after a heated argument, he turned on the group and fired five of their leaders, an action which incited the ensuing turmoil, labeled a strike. Shoriki was ready to stand firm for his beliefs, no matter what the consequences.

The Yomiuri strike gave the unions an early opportunity to gauge the new democratization process advocated by SCAP in a setting that would influence management-labor relations on a national scale. Over a seven-week period from mid-October to early December, 1945, the union controlled the editorial content of the paper, publicizing its demands and denouncing Shoriki as a war criminal. The <u>Yomiuri</u> union demanded collective bargaining, the reinstatement of those fired by the imperious Shoriki, and, influenced by the communists, the rights of the workers to share in the company.[17]

While Shoriki was a strong-willed individualist protecting his rights as owner of the paper, he was also concerned for the welfare of his employees. He still acted as the lord of the domain protecting his family of retainers. In 1943 he had contributed <u>Yomiuri</u> stock worth a million and a half yen to a benefit fund for his workers. Now, despite the management-labor strife, he continued the business operations of the paper so that all the workers, including the strikers, could be paid.

Impetus for a settlement of the strike took an ominous turn on December 3, 1945, when SCAP named Shoriki a war criminal suspect. He was ordered to report to Sugamo Prison on December 12. In the few remaining days before that date an agreement with the union was hammered out: Shoriki would resign and his nominee would become president; he would dispose of all his shares in excess of 30 percent; collective bargaining was agreed to. This was not the end of labor troubles at <u>Yomiuri</u>, which went through another strike in 1946, but for Shoriki it was all he could do. He now faced his own personal threat.

With the stoic passiveness of many Japanese, Shoriki entered Sugamo Prison resigned to accept whatever fate would bring. He was incarcerated as a suspected war criminal. Over the next twenty-one months, aside from the daily degrading tasks of mopping floors and cleaning toilet facilities, he studied Zen Buddhism, daily spending hours meditating in his prison cell. He was interrogated twice during that period and finally released in September, 1947. There was no evidence presented against him, no charges rendered, and no trial. Why was he imprisoned? There is no definitive answer, other than the context of the times and an earnest attempt by the occupation authorities to do their duty. The furor at the Yomiuri and the accusations of the union probably influenced the SCAP action.

Shoriki was not embittered by his prison experience. He was still purged and could not run for public office or actively participate at the Yomiuri, and he was already past sixty, but he did not think of retiring. Instead, he looked for new venues to pursue. His name continued to command great respect among the political and business elite.

In 1949 he became Japan's baseball commissioner as president of the Japan Professional Baseball League.

He was instrumental in starting several successful ventures, including a race track, a motorcycling course, a radio station, and an agency for artists and entertainers. He also began to study a new media, something called television.

At a time when the radio manufacturers were still using vacuum tubes, Shoriki foresaw the tremendous potential for television broadcasting. He organized a television company, Nihon Television Network (NTV), raising 800 million yen in stock subscriptions to finance the undertaking. Soon after the purge ended in August, 1951, he applied for a TV broadcasting license, which was granted in mid-1952, Japan's first. The new medium needed a marketing promotion to catch the fancy of the public and Shoriki responded. He put large television sets in public places for audiences to watch free. It was an instant success, with the TV sets attracting thousands of viewers. The television boom had begun for the broadcasting, advertising, and electronics industries. There were soon seven other commercial television stations, as well as the national broadcasting network, Nihon Hoso Kyokai, in operation. Consumers considered TV sets, first black-and-white and then color, a priority purchase.

Shoriki believed that television became a national morale booster for the Japanese, in addition to its entertainment and commercial success. "I urge underdeveloped countries to start color telecasting as soon as possible for the sake of raising their national prestige and developing their economy," he said. He thought TV could be used as a valuable tool for promoting international friendship, and he offered technical assistance by NTV to countries requesting it.

The most popular TV broadcasts in the postwar era were the baseball games of Shoriki's Tokyo Giants, which were the strongest team at that time. Interestingly, although the league rules allowed each professional team to use two foreign players, and many American ex-major league players performed for Japanese clubs, for several years the Giants did not have any foreigners on their roster. The Giants remained "pure" in what was considered the golden era of Japanese baseball.

When the Martial Virtues Association was revived in March, 1954, Shoriki again supported what it stood for: a healthy military spirit among the nation's young people. He became vice president of the association.

In 1955, Shoriki turned to politics and ran successfully as an independent candidate for the Diet. He was appointed a minister without portfolio under Prime Minister Ichiro Hatoyama (who had also been purged) in 1956 and became the first director of the Japan Atomic Energy Commission, as well as director general of the Hokkaido Development Agency. He also served in the cabinet of Prime Minister Nobusuke Kishi until retiring in 1959.

In 1964 the government awarded Matsutaro Shoriki the First Class Order of the Rising Sun. Upon his death in 1969, he was honored posthumously with the Order of the Rising Sun with Paulownia Flowers.[18]

Shoriki's career as a businessman combined entrepreneurial risk with service to his country. Purged, imprisoned, but still capable and willing to start anew, he was just one of many prewar figures, steeped in the traditional culture, who returned to leadership positions. Any stigma that might have attached to him because of the purge, due to a postwar aversion by the public to the past militaristic policy, was washed away in the fervor of the rebuilding process.

Aside from such established figures as Shoriki, new entrepreneurs also began to appear on the scene. In the postwar years the rigid bounds of prewar society and the proper order of doing things (junjo) were upset by democratization, creating opportunities for those with ability and the right spirit. It was an era when men without the right university degree or family connections could use their innate skills to succeed. Masaru Ibuka, a past president of Sony Corporation, likened it to the sengoku jidai in Japanese history (the period of civil wars in the sixteenth century) when a "proper" background was less important than a man's ability.[19]

The humble beginnings of Giichi Sugimoto

exemplify one entrepreneur whose background offered little more than the Hagakure and military training.[20]

Born to a poor family living in Tokyo, as a child Sugimoto was sent to Fukushima to live with his grandmother, who survived by doing wage labor on nearby farms. He attended primary school there. Sugimoto's memories of those years are of being bullied by older boys because of his Tokyo accent and of being teased as a crybaby. When he fought back and was able to beat other boys his grandmother, who depended on the goodwill of the local farmers for work, would go to their families and apologize for his unruly behavior.

In middle school his teacher taught the class the Hagakure. The strength of the samurai code captured young Giichi's imagination. He adopted it fully, developing a strong belief in the traditional Japanese spirit. Kendo training during his school days helped create a strong, disciplined body.

As a 15-year-old navy recruit in 1944, Sugimoto was eager to fight for his country. He was ready for the first year of martial arts training, calisthenics, bayonet drills, and night fighting exercises, and for the technical classes that would prepare him as a sailor. He was motivated to study hard and finished fourth in a class of eight hundred. In addition, he endured the brutality of the imperial navy's training.

For growing teenage recruits, wartime shortages

allowed only limited rations while the physical exercise they underwent increased their appetites. Sugimoto and his buddies were continually hungry. There were strict orders against going through the garbage for leftovers, but it was done anyway. One night, after using the latrine, Sugimoto heard sounds outside, near the garbage cans. He himself had never searched the garbage for scraps, but he knew that others did. He went to look and recognized a fellow recruit picking out <u>okoge</u> (scorched grains of rice). The recruit realized he was seen and sneaked off in the dark. Just at that moment the squad leader appeared and Sugimoto was caught. There was no way to explain what he was doing there without implicating the other recruit, a terrible breach of honor. Sugimoto would have to face the punishment himself. The next evening, before the assembled barracks troop, he was hung by his wrists to an overhead rafter and beaten with a heavy wooden stick. When he lost consciousness, he was revived, and beaten unconscious again.

Sometime after the incident the other recruit, burdened with guilt, became neurotic and confessed. The squad leader invited Sugimoto to his house, bowed to him, and commended Sugimoto for his proper military spirit in accepting the ordeal. Despite the intense pain and humiliation Sugimoto suffered through he thought the squad leader had acted properly, according to the orders of obedience.   He was also touched by the loyalty of the squad leader to him. Although he had been a victim of severe punishment, Sugimoto was impressed by the spirit of bushido.

The young man dreamed of being a fighter pilot. He would have given his life gladly in the best of samurai traditions.   The reality was a posting to a supply depot in Korea. When the war ended a few months later he was truly disappointed.   He returned to his family on the outskirts of Tokyo where his father ran a small blacksmithing and dray shop.   With no other prospects, and only minimum education, at age sixteen his first job was cleaning the stables.   From that he graduated to leading a horse and wagon, offering transportation and hauling services. His job was to load and unload the wagon, guide the horse through the pot holed streets of Tokyo to make deliveries, and feed and look after the horse.

For Sugimoto opportunity came in many forms. He began collecting scrap while walking his rounds. He straightened pieces of corrugated roofing and resold it; he repaired small motors. He fed the horse well to give it the strength to pull bigger, heavier loads, and was able to do better than other draymen. In a few years the young man realized that trucks were carrying more cargo than horses. He suggested to his father that they buy a truck. When his father declined, Sugimoto was given permission to leave the family business and strike out on his own. He did so, starting his own company by borrowing a friend's three-wheel truck to haul coal cinders. He sold the cinders to residents who used the material to repair the roads in front of their homes and shops.

Sugimoto's simple plan was to work hard, satisfy his customers, and treat his employees well. The plan worked. He took on many different jobs, including road repair, land reclamation, surplus sales, machine brokerage, carpentry and building. By 1987 Giichi Sugimoto's companies were well established in the transportation, recycling, and construction fields, and also held valuable real estate. Sugimoto Industries employed eighty-eight people, all hired for lifetime employment.

He put great effort and care into providing services for his customers, completing projects on time and under budget, whenever possible. "I always taught my employees 'do your work for the customer's satisfaction and joy,'" he explained.

Sugimoto summarized his philosophy by saying, "Once I work with a person, I don't want to say goodbye. Therefore, I don't employ anyone who is not sure to stay with me for 45 years. . . . I seek a deep heartfelt relationship with my employees. It is also an expression of my desire to share both joys and hardships together with them." To foster a company-as-a-family spirit, Sugimoto has purchased the land for homes and constructed houses for his employees, providing them at low cost and with the necessary financing. He and all his employees make "study tours" overseas every two years, visiting different countries and cultures. Sugimoto Industries pays all the expenses.

In addition to Matsutaro Shoriki and Giichi Sugimoto, a whole generation of businessmen emerged steeped in the same bushido culture. Management expert M.Y. Yoshino reported in 1968 that "from analysis of the backgrounds of Japan's present day managerial elite, one factor stands out: they are, as a whole quite homogeneous as to age, educational background, and work experience."[21] Even the late, urbane jet-setter, Akio Morita, who succeeded Ibuka as president of Sony, admitted to being influenced by his military training.   Morita, a physics major in college, underwent the training to become a navy pilot. The war ended before he could join the fleet.   "In the navy," he said, "I had hard training, even though I only had to undergo four months of it in boot camp, but every morning we had to run a long way before breakfast. In those days I did not think of myself as a physically strong person, and yet under such training I found I was not weak after all, and the knowledge of my own ability gave me confidence in myself that I did not have before. It is the same with mental discipline; unless you are forced to use your mind, you become mentally lazy and you will never fulfill your potential."

In the postwar period, young people were not getting the same upbringing, according to Morita. It disturbed him that the education available for his children did not pursue the right values. He said, "where my children were concerned, I felt very strongly that the new postwar educational system in Japan lacked discipline. The teachers, with some important exceptions, did not have the dignity they once had and were not given the status they should have in society." For those reasons Morita's son and daughter were educated in private schools overseas."[22]

Just as their forefathers had done, Japan's postwar industrialists went abroad to bring back new methods and technology. Soichiro Honda bought the best machines he could find overseas; Konosuke Matsushita purchased patents and made licensing agreements; Sony paid for the rights to the transistor.

Also significant in carrying the rebuilding efforts forward were several organizations which acted as powerful lobbies for the postwar business community. These included the influential Federation of Economic Organizations (Keidanren), comprised of trade associations and hundreds of major corporations; the Federation of Employers' Associations (Nikkeiren), and the Committee for Economic Development (Keizai Doyukai). The ideologies set out by these groups made it clear that the responsibilities of management went beyond just showing a profit; that there was a social responsiblity to employees and the public, and to the nation as a whole.[23]

A management-science boom started In the mid-1950s, with government and economic association sponsored industry groups traveling to the United States and Europe for seminars, factory visits, and study tours. Lectures on management controls and quality assurance proliferated.   Deming's total quality management, "just-in-time" inventory, and quality circles were all adopted in this period.   The media contributed to the boom by making business techniques, procedures, and success stories popular reading.

Corporations set out their philosophies for doing business to include a benefit to society, as well as a profit-making goal.   Typical of these is the "Matsushita way," first developed by the late Konosuke Matsushita, the highly respected founder of Matsushita Electric.   It includes service to the nation, fairness, harmony and cooperation, constant improvement in conditions, courtesy and humility, adjustment and assimilation with the world, and gratitude.[24]   Matsushita's hand picked successor, Toshihiko Yamashita, who served as president of the company from 1977 to 1986, followed those guidelines carefully. Yamashita described a good company as ". . . one whose products, policies, and employees have earned the community's respect.   Every employee must be sensitive to what society expects from the enterprise, and must be constantly alert to changing values and needs. This is a corporation's moral duty. A company can survive only by doing work esteemed by society."[25]

The postwar businessmen were motivated to revive their country, as well as to make a living. The thoughts of the Meiji period samurai lived again in a new restoration.   Applied to the business world, the samurai spirit meant creating a strong economy, one that could compete and protect Japan.   This chauvinistic attitude was eventually succeeded by the popular theme of "internationalization," meant to broaden and strengthen Japan's ties to the rest of the world.   Japan responded to western culture in the Meiji period and again in the post Pacific War period, both times in uniquely Japanese fashion, using the motto "western technology-Japanese spirit."

By October 1991 it was no longer necessary to take one's life to assume responsibility for a business failure or a bad investment.   Instead, a resignation and statement of apology became the accepted, if not common, practice in the business world. Kaneo Nakamura, a widely respected executive and chairman of the prestigious Industrial Bank of Japan, resigned following revelations of the bank's involvement in a loan scandal.

Nakamura himself had nothing to do with the shady

proceedings, but defined his action as "the samurai-like thing to do."   He needed to openly express his sincerity. He explained that "it was necessary to show senior and junior people at the bank that they have to take hard decisions if they are to restore the bank's image." Nakamura, who did graduate studies at Harvard Business School, added, "this is very Japanese, and has nothing to do with Harvard style decision making."[26]

Interaction with the outside world--mastery of foreign languages and cultures, thousands of Japanese living and traveling abroad, scores of foreign laborers entering the country from Southeast Asia--has aided the internationalization process. Yet the actions of such sophisticated businessmen as Kaneo Nakamura show the strong identification of the Japanese with their homeland and its traditional culture, assuring that the samurai spirit will continue.

Notes - Chapter 8

1. Miyamoto, Matao. "The Position and Role of Family Business in the Development of the Japanese Company System," Family Business in the Era of Industrial Growth, ed. Akio Okochi and Shigeaki Yasuoka (Tokyo: University of Tokyo Press, 1984), 46.

2. Hirschmeier, Johannes and Tsunehiko Yui. The Development of Japanese Business (Cambridge: Harvard University Press, 1975), 76.

3. 3.Hirschmeier, Johannes. "Shibusawa Eiichi: Industrial Pioneer," The State and Economic Enterprise in Japan, ed. William W. Lockwood (Princeton: Princeton University Press, 1965), 219. Hirschmeier, Shibusawa, 218.

4. Hirschmeier, Development of Japanese Business, 109.

5. Hirschmeier, Shibusawa, 226.

6. Hirschmeier,

7. Shibusawa, 225.

8. Yamamura, Kozo. "The Founding of Mitsubishi: A

Case Study in Japanese Business History," <u>Business History Review</u>, Vol. XLI, No.2 (Summer 1967), 158.

9.   Ibid., 141.

10. Yamamura, Kozo. "Zaibatsu, Prewar and Zaibatsu, Postwar," <u>Journal of Asian Studies</u>, Vol. XXIII, No.4 (Aug. 1964), 540-541.

11. Baerwald, Hans H. <u>The Purge of Japanese Leaders Under the Occupation</u> (Berkeley: University of California Press, 1959), 98.

12. Cohen, Theodore. <u>Remaking Japan</u> (New York: The Free Press, 1987), 154.

13. Ibid., 354.

14. Baerwald, 78-80.

15. Ibid., 154.

16. Uhlan, Edward and Dana L. Thomas. <u>Shoriki, Miracle Man of Japan</u> (New York: Exposition Press, 1957).

17 . Cohen, 241.

18. Unattributed. "Yomiuri Shimbun's Shoriki Dies at 84," <u>Japan Times</u>, Oct. 10, 1969; 4.

19. Rosovsky, Henry and Kozo Yamamura. "Entrepreneurial Studies in Japan: An Introduction," Business History Review, Vol. XLIV, No.1 (Spring 1970), 2-3.

20. Sugimoto, Giichi. Six-Sided Management: Righteousness, Gratitude, Compassion, trans. William Cook (Lewiston, NY: Edwin Mellen Press, 1989).

21. Yoshino, M.Y. Japan's Managerial System, Tradition and Innovation (Cambridge: The MIT Press, 1968), 91.

22. Morita, Akio with Edwin M. Reingold and Mitsuko Shimomura. Made in Japan (New York: E.P. Dutton, 1986), 106.

23. Yoshino, 94-104.

24. Kamioka, Kazuyoshi. Japanese Business Pioneers (Union City, CA: Heian International, 1988), 70-71.

25. Yamashita, Toshihiko. The Panasonic Way, trans. Frank Baldwin (Tokyo: Kodansha International, 1989), 32.

26. Sterngold, James. "Banker Resigns in Japan," in The New York Times, Oct. 23, 1991, C-1.

Chapter 9

OTHER EVENTS

The Japanese themselves recognize the samurai spirit
to the extent that its use has often become overuse and
abuse. In many discrepant ways the spirit is regularly
evoked to simply sharpen one's mental attitude, to fight for
a cause, or for money-making purposes. For example,
management in major companies employ their interpretation
of the spirit to promote hard work, efficiency, and sacrifice
among their employees. The commercialism of the ethos
does not daunt their cause. Some firms create a scenario in
which they protect Japan from what they see as a hostile
world environment. Training of company recruits includes
seishin kyoiku (spiritual training), institutional material,
technical subjects, and often tests of physical endurance.
Anthropologist Thomas P. Rohlen, in his study of a
Japanese bank, found the bank used training methods
borrowed from Zen, the samurai heritage, and other
traditions.[1]

Although spiritual training was considered militaristic
and frowned upon in the immediate postwar years, as the
war memories have faded it has returned to instill the proper

attitudes in today's company employees. Loyalty to fellow employees, to the company, and to the country is a foremost principle in the training.

Government bureaucrats show loyalty by exhibiting an attitude comparable to the samurai code of ethics and elite consciousness. A spirit of "sacrifice for the public good" is cornmon, creating kanryodo (a way of the bureaucrat). Political scientist Chalmers Johnson, one of America's foremost Japanologists, credited the latent power of the government's "samurai sword" for preventing people from questioning the authority of the bureaucracy. There is a popular consciousness and acceptance of authority in Japan, which avoids adversarial situations leading to litigation and penalties. The "spirit" exhibited by ministries such as the Ministry of International Trade and Industry (MITI) is characterized as "nationalistic". The bureaucrats main thrust is to protect Japanese industries from foreign pressure.[2] In the recent Daiwa Bank scandal, which involved unreported trading losses by the bank's New York branch, the role of the Finance Ministry exemplified this situation. The American authorities accused the ministry of attempting to cover up by failing to promptly report Daiwa's losses after learning of them.

As if to emphasize the importance of a proper spirit,

the absence of samurai <u>konjo</u> is just as vital. This lack of the spirit was criticized in February 1972 when a deadly drama captured Japan's attention.   Five leftwing extremists, members of the <u>Rengo Sekigun </u>(United Red Army), barricaded themselves in a resort villa in Karuizawa, seized a female hostage, the wife of the caretaker, and kept over six hundred police at bay for ten days.   The five were part of a group sought for earlier robberies of a post office and a gun shop. The episode finally ended when the police subjected the radicals to an eight-hour barrage of gun fire, tear gas, and water cannons. The radicals returned fire, killing two policemen and wounding fifteen others. The gang of five were captured alive with their remaining firearms and ammunition. Live television coverage carried the action to a rapt nationwide audience.[3]

The United Red Army's leftist political beliefs were too extreme for the conservative majority of Japanese. Their aborted uprising was seen as a revolt against the money centered social structure, and the changes resulting from Japan's rapid buildup of gross national product and industrialization. The public was not ready to embrace such beliefs and to give up the country's hard won economic success.

But the radicals were criticized after the incident, not so

much for their politics, or for their method of attempting to achieve a political revolution, but for not showing sincerity by fighting to their death. In an editorial the mainstream Mainichi Shimbun said they did not show a proper Japanese spirit.[4] Whatever their radical beliefs, whatever the actions taken to achieve them, the guilty could have been forgiven by the Mainichi, and the millions of readers the newspaper influences, if the revolutionists had exhibited the proper spirit. If they had acted as samurai showing loyalty to their cause; if they showed bravery in the face of the police, and if they exhibited a willingness to die, they would have been respected. Instead they were ridiculed. (In addition, a generational gap in beliefs also emerged soon after when in remorse the father of one of the radicals hanged himself following his son's arrest.)[5]

Steinhoff, in her study of the internal dynamics of the United Red Army, concluded that the revolutionaries were really conventional in their management practices. They could easily have fit right into corporate Japan or a government agency as well trained employees.[6]

Despite the United Red Army's avoidance of death in battle-- they made a practice of taking hostages and using coercion--there are instances where the final sacrifice is made.

Early in the morning of Tuesday, March 23, 1976, two small planes took off from Chofu Airfield, outside Tokyo. The young pilot and sole occupant of one plane appeared to be a wartime kamikaze pilot. He wore a military uniform complete with silk scarf, goggles, gloves, and a rising sun emblem. In the other plane rode a team of photographers who were to take general air action shots to publicize an upcoming movie. The two planes circled briefly before the kamikaze waved off and flew toward a residential area in Tokyo's posh Setagaya district. Actor Mitsuharu Maeno, whose career had been limited to "B" movies and an appearance in a porno flick, set course on his last flight, determined to die a glorious death.

Maeno's destination was the home of Yoshio Kodama, an influential figure deeply implicated in the Lockheed bribery scandal. Through Kodama's offices, Lockheed had distributed thousands of dollars in bribes to ensure that its aircraft would be selected by the Japanese Air Self-Defense Force. To Maeno, an ultrarightist, the image of the JSDF and the honor of Japan were at stake. The underhanded tactics Kodama used to influence, and possibly weaken, the defense of the country made Maeno emotionally distraught.

Maeno had previously scouted the area and soon spotted Kodama's large, luxurious home from the air. He cut the airplane engine off and pushed the controls forward to shift into a dive. At Chofu Airport radio operators heard his last words, "Tenno Heika, Banzai" (Long Live the Emperor!). Moments later the plane crashed into the second floor of Kodama's home, starting a fire. Firemen later found Maeno's charred body in the wreckage. Kodama, who was in another wing of the building, escaped unharmed. Maeno had sacrificed his life in the role of a kamikaze pilot, ostensibly to protect the country. A police search of Maeno's apartment turned up many of Yukio Mishima's works, confirming the influence of Japan's renowned postwar samurai.[7]

Although most newspapers and political commentators at the time labeled the incident as absurd and incomprehensible, others found that Maeno's actions were understandable. Akira Fukushima, a professor of criminal psychiatry with the Tokyo Medical and Dental College, wrote in the prestigious Asahi Journal, "to my mind, Maeno was hardly abnormal or exceptional, let alone insane. He was a typical representative of our younger generation."[8]

Fukushima believed that the modern Japanese society of material abundance, the image culture of television, and Maeno's indulgent parents had created a narcissist, prodigal son with an urge to commit suicide. Maeno's patriotic love of the Emperor, the affinity he felt with Yukio Mishima, and his desire to demonstrate "real samurai spirit" dictated his actions. The <u>tokkotai</u> uniform he wore allowed the actor to become a patriotic martyr on behalf of the Japanese nation.

Fukushima also blamed Japan's educational system, which drills students with facts and figures but fails to give them the tools to make valid ideological choices. Expanding the thought, Fukushima pointed out the attraction to modern day youth of new religions, farcical faith, or extreme radicalism, almost presaging the current Aum Shinri Kyo debacle.

The Lockheed scandal also produced an act of extreme loyalty by Prime Minister Kakuei Tanaka's chauffeur. During the criminal investigation of the affair Masanori Kasahara, 42, committed suicide rather than tell the police where he had driven the prime minister on certain days. Kasahara made his supreme sacrifice to protect his lord.

In the wake of the Recruit companies' stock payoff, manipulation, and insider information scandal, Prime Minister Noboru Takeshita's former secretary Ihei Aoki slashed one wrist and hanged himself. Aoki's action did not help Takeshita escape the Recruit scandal though as the prime minister was forced to resign.

Other adherents of the samurai spirit followed a less spectacular and less self-destructive path, but one filled with sacrifice and dedication. Gichin Funakoshi, considered the father of modern karate-do, became a living example of a spartan samurai existence until his death in 1957. His autobiography, detailing his rise from a small village in Okinawa to later eminence as a karate master became a best seller. Funakoshi promoted the virtues of a life dedicated to the bushido spirit. His basic tenets for practicing and understanding karate became guidelines for daily living, extolling such traits as seriousness of purpose, self-motivation, modesty, awareness of others' good points, and following the rules of ethics in daily life.[9]

Masutatsu Oyama has practiced, taught, and written about karate for more than fifty years. As the founder of his own school and president of the International Karate Organization, he advocates moderation, control, and restraint to go with the martial arts. "A true warrior is also a true gentleman," he has said. "Japan's greatest virtue is the spirit of the martial arts. . . Forever and a day I continue on the way of the warrior, unchanged. I am determined to restore the true warrior spirit.[10]

International Budo University, founded in 1984, in

Katsuura, Chiba Prefecture, provides a formal education for the modern warrior. Applicants must have already attained a grade (dan) in judo or kendo and be prepared to continue in martial arts while taking courses in business and liberal arts. University president Shigeyoshi Matsumae ably represents the spirit and tradition taught to the prewar generation. He is a past president of the International Judo Federation[11] and also held the position of chief of the general affairs section of the ultranationalistic Imperial Rule Assistance Association.

The film industry added liberally to the images of the samurai and the yakuza, but it cannot compare to the spirit achieved by the imaginative writers of manga (comics). The series "Silent Service," published by Comic Morning magazine, sold more than two million volumes as a book through 1989. This spectacular tale told the story of a Japanese super submarine, equipped with nuclear technology and weapons, which became an independent nation during a conflict with the United States and the Soviet Union. Submarine commander Shiro Kaieda and his crew exhibited all the attributes of righteous warriors.[12] Fanciful and imaginative, the cartoon series transmitted the image of the samurai spirit to daily readers dressed in business suits and packed into commuter trains. For a few moments strap hangers could forget the stress of another day and dream of valiant modern warfare. Diet member Shintaro Ishihara, co-author of <u>The Japan That Can Say No</u>, commented that, "to say the least, for me this is an exceedingly sweet and dangerous <u>manga</u>, but one that I cannot keep my eyes off."[13]

In all these pockets of society the samurai spirit still pulsates steadily. At times the public's attitude toward the samurai code appears confused. While popular movies, novels, and cartoons offer fictionalized caricatures, produced in search of quick profits--and in effect demean the samurai heritage of the country--the concept of loyalty continues as a cherished virtue and the proper spirit earns praise. The role of the samurai appears to have a permanent place in the national character beyond that attributed to the battles of the yakuza and the violence of the left and right radicals. It is embedded deep in the national identity, bonded to the soul of the country. The samurai spirit in postwar Japan endures, if not in military battles, then in the world of economic warfare, or just simply in the toil of the common man performing a mundane task in a dutiful manner.

Perhaps the most allegorical expression of the samurai

spirit in postwar Japan was the simplest: the crack of the bat in the hands of home run king Sadaharu Oh. The star baseball player's powerful stroke was developed by practicing iai nuki (art of withdrawing and replacing the sword).

A superb batsman and star of the Yomiuri Tokyo Giants for twenty-two seasons, Oh hit a world record 868 homeruns during his career. From 1959 when he joined the Giants to 1980 when he retired, his exploits were reported in detail in the nation's general print media, radio and television, and of course the sports newspapers and magazines. His stance, his unusual raised-leg swing, his follow thru, his mental attitude all became topics of discussion by media experts and fanatic followers of the sport.

Before Oh graduated from Waseda Commercial High School in Tokyo his name was well known to the nation's sports fans. Baseball scouts spotted him as having professional potential from his early junior high school days. In high school he led his team as a pitcher and a hitter, and was considered the best schoolboy player in Japan.

While in high school he also showed the stoic heroism of the samurai, both by playing with painful injuries when his team needed him, and by being denied the opportunity to play in the National Amateur Athletic Competition (Kokutai). The rules for this tournament, as interpreted by the governing officials, decreed that it was for Japanese only. Although Oh was born and raised in Tokyo, his father was Chinese and under Japanese law that made him Chinese also. The ruling authorities declared him ineligible to play. At Oh's insistence the team went on to play without him.

With most of the pro teams bidding for his services, Oh signed with the Giants because that was the team he had followed from boyhood. The Giants offered less money than some other teams, but in his heart Oh felt that he had always wanted to be a Tokyo Giant. From age 18 he joined the professional world of baseball only to discover how raw his talents were, how much work and training he needed to polish his skills.

After three mediocre seasons in which he hit just 7, 17, and 13 homeruns, the fans and sportswriters speculated openly about his supposed star quality. Oh himself realized he had not reached his full potential. He underwent Zen spiritual training and sword practice--all duly reported by the Japanese media--to become a successful baseball player. The results were miraculous. Starting in 1962, for 15 of the next 16 seasons Oh led the league in homeruns, eventually surpassing Babe Ruth's (714) and Hank Aaron's

(755) lifetime records. He was selected most valuable player nine times.[14]

The symbol of the bat as a sword comes easily. The illusion is one that millions of Japanese followed daily throughout Oh's career. A modern day hero evolved who was committed to the concepts of the ancient samurai. In the dream world of baseball fans the samurai spirit lived on.

In the world of sports, the 1964 Tokyo Olympic Games provided bittersweet memories for the Japanese. The fact that the Olympics were awarded to Tokyo just 19 years after the end of the War was a source of tremendous national pride. The event provided an opportunity to rejoin the world community as a peaceful nation. Seemingly unlimited government spending went into broadening the streets, building apartment blocks to be used first as an Olympic village and then as public housing, modernizing the sewage system, constructing a monorail and new subway lines to replace the prewar streetcars, and many other projects. Homeowners were given incentives to modernize their plumbing and install flush toilets, businesses were urged to join Olympic support groups, and whole communities were encouraged to decorate their streets and the route of the Olympic flame as it was carried on its way to Tokyo.

Perhaps the one event of the Games which might have best symbolized a fighting spirit, but instead became a national disappointment, for the Japanese occurred in the marathon on Wednesday, October 21, 1964. The world's ranking marathoner, Abebe Bikila of Ethiopia, the winner in 1960, led a strong field of foreign runners, including Ron Clarke of Australia; Ron Hill, Brian Kilby and Basil Heatley of England, and Buddy Edelen of the U.S. None of the Japanese entrants was expected to finish among the medal winners.

The runners gathered at one o'clock in the Olympic Stadium for the gunshot to start the 42-kilometer trek. They circled the track once and then poured out of the stadium along the streets packed with spectators for 20 kilometers before turning and heading back. Bikila, who had been operated on for acute appendicitis just five weeks earlier, assumed the lead at the 20- K mark. Gaunt and determined, the Ethiopian army sergeant ran steadily, his bare feet gliding over the pavement at a record pace.

As three o'clock approached other track and field events came to a standstill. The anticipation of the crowd of 80,000 inside the stadium grew as they heard the growing roar of the thousands lining the streets outside. The first finishers approached. Through the tunnel entrance came a lone, thin, dark- skinned man striding upright around the track to the finish. Bikila completed the marathon in two hours, 12 minutes, and then did a calisthenics stretching routine in the infield. He was fit and in fine form despite having just run the 42 kilometers in record time. But where were the others? There was a momentary lull before any other runners came into view. Then the cheers could be heard again from outside, even louder this time.

Army Lt. Kokichi Tsuburaya entered the stadium to a thunderous ovation. A Japanese runner coming in second in the marathon! But Tsuburaya's appearance epitomized the struggle of the marathon. He labored forward, close to exhaustion. He had done his best, yet there were still a few hundred meters to go. His legs moved mechanically without drive as he attempted to finish the last lap. Another competitor, Basil Heatley of England, appeared about 30 meters behind Tsuburaya. The crowd urged, pleaded, and cheered for Tsuburaya to pick up his pace as he slogged along the back stretch. He could not respond. Heatley surged and moved closer and the crowd shouted pleadingly at Tsuburaya. Their voices could not make his body move any faster. At the far turn Heatley overtook him, lengthened his lead down the stretch and finished second for the silver medal. Just 3.6 seconds later Tsuburaya came in to claim the bronze medal for Japan. He immediately collapsed on the infield grass and required medical attention.

Physically, Tsuburaya soon recovered from the shock of his "loss", even though a third place finish for Japan marked a truly great achievement. But the nation which saw him slip from second to third in the last few moments did not recover as quickly. The media critics and commentators discussed the issue as if the so- called unique Japanese spirit had been broken. Tsuburaya had been overtaken on the home stretch with his countrymen urging him on. How could it have happened?   In the weeks and months following, Tsuburaya's training methods, his personal life, the food in the army, all became subjects for debate. The Olympic Games became the peak of Tsuburaya's career. A year later, unable to adjust his personal life to the stigma of his Olympic performance, he committed suicide, as much a victim of the Japanese spirit as any samurai.

The 1964 games also marked the first time that judo made an appearance as an official sport in the Olympics. The Japanese considered judo one of their own traditional sports. In the predicted medal counts, the experts gave the judo medals, including the gold, to the Japanese. This, too, proved to be a national disappointment when the great

Dutch judoka Anton Geesink defeated Japan's Akio Kaminaga in the heavyweight finals.

The exploits of mountain climber Naomi Uemura and sailor Kenichi Horie were also considered conquests only achievable by those who are spiritually strong. Uemura climbed the highest peaks of each continent over several years before perishing on Mt. Whittier in Alaska. Horie sailed across the Pacific alone from Japan to the west coast of the U.S., then later repeated the feat by sailing west from the U.S. to Japan. Newspaper accounts of both men's successes gave credit to their strong spirit.

In sports, whether individual or team, there can only be one winner. Keeping score of wins or losses en route to a glorious championship or a disastrous defeat is not part of the code, although the public would fondly embrace it as such. The samurai spirit is not restricted to either winners or losers, but is there to enhance the way the game is played.

Notes - Chapter 9

1. Rohlen, Thomas P.

2. Johnson, Chalmers. MITI and the Japanese Miracle (Stanford: Stanford University Press, 1982) 39, 81.

3. See Japan Times (20 - 29 Feb., 1972), daily news reports, articles on events related to this incident.

4. Hisashi Inoue, "As New Leader, Japan Needs to Confront the Past Honestly," Japan Times, weekly international edition (24 Sept. 1990).

5. "Radical's Father Hangs Himself," Japan Times (29 Feb. 1972), 2.

6. Steinhoff, Patricia G. "Hijackers, Bombers, and Bank Robbers: Managerial Style in the Japanese Red Army," Journal of Asian Studies, Vol. 48, No.4 (Nov. 1989), 738.

7. "Movie Actor Does 'Kamikaze' Attack," Japan Times (24 March 1976), 1.

8. Fukushima, Akira. "Suicidal Attack on the Kodama Mansion," The Japan Interpreter, Vol. XI, No.1 (Spring, 1976), 71.

9. Funakoshi, Gichin. Karate-Do My Way of Life(Tokyo: Kodansha International, 1975).

10. Quoted in "Karate: My Life for 50 Years," Japan Quarterly, 30 (1983), 420-422, from an interview which appeared in Asahi Journal.

11. Catalog, International Budo University, 1990.

12. Karl Schoenberger, "Japan's 'Manga' Fantasies: Military Bolts Into 'Comic' Action," <u>Los Angeles Times</u> (23 Oct. 1990), H2.

13. Ibid., quoted from a review by Ishihara In the <u>Sankei Shimbun</u>.

14. Oh, Sadaharu and David Falkner. <u>Sadaharu Oh, A Zen Way of Baseball</u> (New York: Vintage Books, 1978).

Chapter 10

CONCLUSION

The examples of samurai spirit, ranging from the subdued nobility of the Showa Emperor to the forced play-acting of Toshiro Mifune and Ken Takakura, have become role models for the generations born since the end of the Pacific War. In emulating the pure intentions of the past there are sometimes wildly extorted transpositions to encompass kidnapping, murder, and suicide. Interpretations of the samurai spirit have been varied and subjective as the Japanese struggle with their modern world image.

The Emperor, whether Showa or Heisei, still remains the Emperor, steeped in tradition and the background of ancient values. Disregarded by some, considered a useless adjunct to the government by others, for the majority the Emperor continues to symbolize loyalty and the concept of giri, while actively practicing rituals of the former state religion of Shinto. Although the reign of Emperor Heisei has been less formal, the imperial monarchy still carries with it the dignity and radiant influence of the supposedly unique Japanese spirit.

For the laborer or the leader, the spirit may surface in feelings of obligation or loyalty, or as a sacrifice for the good of a business group, a suicide generated by shame or depression, or a resignation. These are the marks of life more likely to touch today's Japanese.

The need to stoically meet a hardship or to prove one's loyalty to a person or cause is not likely to occur with any regularity. When it does, however, the samurai heritage is there embedded in the national character, somewhere within the heart and soul of each being, waiting to be called upon.

In a sense the samurai spirit represents Japan just as the independence of the western cowboy represents the United States, or the haughty colonialist reign of the British empire marks the history of that country. In each nation vestiges of the cultural background are still reflected, but perhaps none so markedly as the samurai.

In this current period of so-called internationalization for Japan the transition of values to those of the West lags behind. While industry has been able to quickly transition to high technology to compete on a global scale, a code of conduct for the populace is still evolving. The study of the Japanese being (Nihonjinron) continues. Some traditions have been cast away, while others will not die so easily.

As the examples of the Emperor and MacArthur, Lt. Onoda and his devotion to duty, Mishima in his ritualistic suicide, and others have shown, the active samurai among the Japanese have been moved to action in a variety of ways. Their behavior may seem incongruous in the context of Japan's postwar democracy, but they acted with the same loyalty and bravery as existed in feudal times. By strict definition their conduct may not be in accordance with the samurai code, yet they are reminders that embers of the spirit are still alive.

But beyond the samurai-like actions of these relatively few, the reaction by the general public attests to continued admiration for their deeds.   Each act rekindles a spirit that refuses to die. In the popular literature, TV and movies the heroes adopt the values that the Japanese believe are theirs.

While much of the heritage is admirable, in the controversy in 1995 over a Diet resolution to apologize for the war, the resoluteness of the Pacific War soldier came to fore. The faction opposed to an apology, led by the Association of Bereaved Families, Shintoists, and the rightwing ultranationalists, emphasized devotion to the Emperor and the cause of the souls of those who died for the nation's cause. Their successful effort to squash an official apology tied nationalism to pieces of the national ethos and with it the samurai credo. Unfortunately, the purity of the samurai spirit became enmeshed in a political morass.

Instead, the samurai spirit should be remembered as a symbol of national pride, valor, loyalty, and honor, not for the abuse it has suffered or the sometimes shameful ends it has met in modern Japan.

BIBLIOGRAPHY

Primary

Aida, Yuji. <u>Prisoner of the British</u> (London: The Cresset Press, 1966).

Emperor Meiji. <u>Imperial Rescript on Education</u>. Tokyo, 1890.

Emperor Showa <u>Imperial Rescript</u>, Jan. 1, 1946, trans.

U.S. Dept. of Army, SCAP, "Political Reorientation of Japan" (Washington, D.C.: Government Printing Office, 1949).

Fukuzawa, Yukichi. <u>The Autobiography of Fukuzawa Yukichi</u>, trans. Eiichi Kiyooka (New York: Columbia University, 1966).

Funakoshi, Gichin. <u>Karate-Do My Way of Life</u> (Tokyo: Kodansha International, 1975).

Onoda, Hiroo. <u>No Surrender, My Thirty Year War</u>, trans. Charles S. Terry (Tokyo: Kodansha International Ltd., 1974).

MacArthur, Douglas A. <u>Reminiscences</u> (New York: McGraw- Hill, 1964).

Mishima, Yukio. "An Appeal," <u>The Japan Interpreter</u>, trans. Harris I. Martin (Winter 1971).

Confessions of a Mask, trans. Meredith Weatherby (New York: New Directions Publishing Co., 1958).

Death in Midsummer and Other Short Stories, trans. Geoffrey W. Sargent (New York: New Directions Books, 1966).

Hagakure Nyumon (The Way of the Samurai), trans. Kathryn Sparling (New York: Putnam Publishing Group, 1983).

"Patriotism," ESquire, trans. Geoffrey W. Sargent (Apr. 1966)

Sun & Steel, trans. John Bester (Tokyo: Kodansha International Ltd., 1970).

" Tate no Kai," The Japan Interpreter, trans. Andrew Horvat (Winter 1971).

The Temple of the Golden Pavilion, trans. Ivan Morris (New York: Alred A. Knopf, Inc., 1959). \

"Testament of a Samurai," Sports Illustrated, trans. Michael Gallagher (11 Jan. 1971).

"Yang-Ming Thought as Revolutionary Philosophy," The Japan Interpreter, trans. Harris I. Martin (Winter 1971).

Yamamoto, Tsunetomo. Hagakure, recorded by Tashiro Tsuramoto, trans. William Scott Wilson (Tokyo: Kodansha International Ltd., 1979).

206

Secondary -- Unpublished

Brown, Allan R. "The Figurehead Role of the Japanese Emperor: Perception and Reality" (Ph.D. diss., Stanford University, 1971).

Ikeda. Matthew S.   " Yukio Mishima : A study of Personal Metamorphosis (Ph.D. diss., University of Chicago, 1974.

Stark, David Harold. "The Yakuza: Japanese Crime Incorporated" (Ph.D. diss., University of Michigan, 1981).

Wilson, Michiko Niikuni. "The Fabrication of Beauty: The Art of Mishima Yukio" (Ph.D. diss., University of Texas, Austin, 1977).

Published

Anderson, Ronald S. Japan, Three Epochs of Modern Education (Washington, D.C.: U.S. Department of Health, Education, and Welfare, 1959).

Asahi Shimbun Correspondents. 28 Years in the Guam Jungle (Tokyo: Asahi Shimbun Publishing Co., 1972)

Bellah, Robert N. Tokugawa Religion (New York: The Free Press, 1957).

Benedict, Ruth. The Chrysanthemum and the Sword (Boston: Houghton Mifflin Co., 1946).

Buehrer, Beverly Bare. Japanese Films (Jefferson, North Carolina: McFarland & Co., 1990).

Buruma, Ian. A Japanese Mirror (London: Jonathon
    Cape Ltd., 1984).

Desser, David. The Samurai Films of Akira Kurosawa
(Ann Arbor, MI: UMI Research Press, 1983).

De Vos, George A. and Wagastuma, Hiroshi. Heritage
of Endurance (Berkeley: University of California Press,
1984).

Earl, David Magarey. Emperor and Nation in Japan
    (Seattle: University of Washington Press, 1964).

Hearn, Lafcadio. Japan, An Attempt at Interpretation.
    (New York: Grosset & Dunlap, 1904).

Iga, Mamoru. The Thorn in the Chrysanthemum
(Berkeley: University of California Press, 1986).

Ito, Masashi. The Emperor's Last Soldiers. (New York:
Coward-McCann Inc., 1967).

James, D. Clayton. The Years of MacArthur, 3 (Boston:
Houghton Mifflin Co., 1985).

Kaplan, David E. and Dubro, Alec. Yakuza (Reading,
    Mass.: Addison-Wesley Publishing Co., 1986).

Kawahara, Toshiaki. Hirohito and His Times (Tokyo:
Kodansha International Ltd., 1990).

Lebra, Takie Sugiyama. Japanese Patterns of Behavior
(Honolulu: University of Hawaii Press, 1976).

Lory, Hillis. Japan's Military Masters (New York: The
    Viking Press, 1943).

Maki, John M., trans. and ed. Japan's Commission on the Constitution: The Final Report (Seattle: University of Washington Press, 1980).

McDonald, Keiko I. Cinema East (East Brunswick, N.J.: Associated University Presses, 1983).

Mellen, Joan. The Waves at Genji's Door (New York: Pantheon Books, 1976).

Minami, Hiroshi. Psychology of the Japanese People, trans. Albert R. Ikoma (Tokyo: University of Tokyo Press, 1971).

Morishima, Michio. Why Has Japan 'Succeeded'? (Cambridge: Cambridge University Press, 1982).

Morris, Ivan. The Nobility of Failure. Rinehart and (New York: Holt, Winston, 1975.

Mosely, Leonard. Hirohito, Emperor of   Japan (New York: Prentice Hall, 1967).

Mounsey, Augustus H. The Satsuma Rebellion (London: John Murray, 1879; reprinted by University Publications of America, Washington, D.C., 1979).

Nathan, John. Mishima, A Biography (Boston: Little, Brown and Co., 1974).

Nitobe, Inazo. Bushido, The Soul of Japan (New York: G.P. Putnam's Sons, 1905).

Osanaga, Kanroji. Hirohito: An Intimate Portrait of

the Japanese Emperor (Los Angeles: Gateway Publishers, Inc., 1975).

Reischauer, Edwin O. The Japanese Today (Cambridge, Mass.: The Belknap Press of Harvard University Press, 1988).

Richie, Donald. Japanese Cinema (Garden City, New York: Doubleday & Co., 1971).

Saga, Junichi. Confessions of a Yakuza (Tokyo: Kodansha Int'l. 1991).

Sansom, Sir George Bailey. A History of Japan, 1615-1867 (Stanford University Press, 1963).

Sato, Tadao. Currents in Japanese Cinema, trans. Gregory Barrett (Tokyo: Kodansha International Ltd., 1982).

Scott-Stokes, Henry. The Life and Death of Yukio Mishima (Toronto: Doubleday Canada Ltd., 1974).

Swinson, Arthur. Four Samurai (London: Hutchinson & Co., 1968).

Takeda, Kiyoko. The Dual Image of the Japanese Emperor (London: MacMillan Education Ltd., 1988).

Tsurumi, Kazuko. Social Change and the Individual (Princeton: Princeton University Press, 1970).

Turnbull, S.R. The Samurai, A Military History (New

York: Macmillan Publishing *Co., 1977).*

United States Department of the Army, SCAP, PoliticalReorientation of Japan, Sept. 1945-Sept. 1948

(Washington, D.C.: Government Printing Office, 1949), trans. Foreign Affairs

Association of Japan, comp., The Japan Yearbook, 1935 (Tokyo: Kenkyusha Press, 1935).

United States War Department. Handbook on Japanese Military Forces (Washington, D.C.: U.S. Government Printing Office, 1944).

Varley, Paul H. with Ivan and Nobuko Morris. Samurai (New York: Delacorte Press, 1970).

Articles

Anonymous. "Emperor Recalls Meeting M'Arthur," Japan Times (26 Aug. 1965).

"Films: Phoenix or Flop?" Japan Quarterly, 19 (1972).

International Film Guide, ed. Peter Cowie (London: The Tantivy Press, 1978).

International Motion Picture Almanac, ed. Barry Monush (New York: Quigley Publishing *Co.,* 1991).

"LDP Discards Motoshima for Nagasaki Mayoral Race," in Japan Times, weekly international edition (11 March 1991).

Minor articles, sidebars. Japan Times (27, 28 Nov.

1970).

"Mishima Commits Ritual Suicide in GSDF Eastern Hq," in <u>Japan Times</u> (26 Nov. 1970).

"Mishima Yukio 1925-1970", A Prologue, <u>Japan Interpreter</u> (Winter 1971).

"Radical's Father Hangs Himself," <u>Japan Times</u> (29 Feb. 1972).

"The Talk of the Town", editorial comments, <u>New Yorker</u> (12 Dec. 1970).

Adams, Robert Martin. "Letter from Tokyo," <u>Hudson Review</u> (Summer 1971).

Brudnoy, D. "Mishima Yukio, RIP," <u>National Review,</u> (29 Dec. 1970).

Coox, Alvin D. "Qualities of Japanese Military Leadership," <u>Journal of Asian History,</u> 2 (1968).

Davis, Don. "The Showa Reign Bracketed Japan's Tragedy and Change," <u>San Diego Union</u> (7 Jan. 1989).

De Vos, George A. with Mizushima, Keiichi. "Organization and Social Function of Japanese Gangs: Historical Development and Modern Parallels," <u>Socialization for Achievement</u> (Berkeley: University of California Press, 1973).

De Vos, George A. with Wagatsuma, Hiroshi. "Minority Status and Delinquency in Japan," <u>Socialization for Achievement</u>.

Desser, David. "Toward a Structural Analysis of the Postwar Samurai Film," Quarterly Review of Film Studies, 8 (1983).

Funabiki, Jon. "Two Hirohito Ceremonies May Show Confusion on Role of Emperor," San Diego Union (11 Jan. 1989).

Hiatt, Fred. "Public Debate of Japan's Emperor System Inhibited Since Hirohito's Death," Washington Post (19 Jan. 1989).

Inoue, Hisashi. "As New Leader, Japan Needs to Confront the Past Honestly," Japan Times, weekly international edition (24 Sept. 1990).

Inouye, Charles Shiro. "Do Non-Japanese Fear the Flame?" The Nation (30 Jan. 1989).

Iwasaki, Akira. "The Battle of the Screens," Japan Quarterly, 4 (1957).

Jansen, Marius B. "Monarchy and Modernization In Japan," Journal of Asian Studies, 36 (1977).

Kirk, Donald. "Crime, Politics and Finger Chopping," New York Times Magazine (12 Dec., 1976).

Krisher, Bernard. "A Talk with the Emperor of Japan," Newsweek (29 Sept. 1975).

Lebra, Joyce C. "Mishima's Last Act," Literature East & West (Winter 1971).

McDonald, Keiko I. "Swordsmanship and Gamesmanship: Historical Kurosawa's Milieu in Yojimbo," Literature/Film Quarterly, 8 (1980).

Morris, Ivan. "Theory and Psychology of Ultra-Nationalism," Sekai (May 1946), Masao Murayama Thought and Behavior in Modern Japanese Politics, ed. Ivan Morris (London: Oxford University Press, 1963) •

Murata, Kiyoaki. "Blood and Tears," Japan Times (3 Aug. 1957).

"The War Saga Boom," Japan Times (8 Dec. 1956).

Naito, Yuko. "Familiarity Breeds Content in Samurai Dramas," Japan Times, weekly international edition (8-14 April 1991).

Niemeyer, Gerhart. "How Stable Is Japan," National Review (15 Dec. 1970).

Richie, Donald. "The State of the Japanese Film," Japan Quarterly, 30 (1983).

"Yukio Mishima--a Reminiscence," Japan Times (2 Dec. 1970).

Sanger, David. "Japan Clings to a Vague, Historic Reverence," New York Times (2 Oct. 1988).

"Japanese Flick on Their TV's and Glimpse Well-Hidden History," New York Times International (9 Jan. 1989).

Schecter, Jerrold. "The Samurai Who Committed Hara-Kiri" <u>Life</u> (11 Dec. 1970).

Schoenberger, Karl. "Japanese Taking Unprecedented Stand Against Yakuza Menace," <u>Japan Times</u> (14 April 1988).

. "Japan's 'Manga' Fantasies: Military Bolts Into 'Comic' Action," <u>Los Angeles Times</u> (23 Oct. 1990), H2.

Schrader, Paul. "Yakuza-Eiga, A Primer," <u>Film Comment</u> (Jan. 1974).

Segers, Frank. "Japanese Bet on New pic 'Black Rain,' and So Do Experts," <u>Variety</u> (3 - 9 May 1989).

Seidensticker, Edward. "Mishima Yukio, " <u>Hudson Review</u> (Summer 1971).

Trumbull, Robert. "A Leader Who Took Japan to War, to Surrender, and Finally to Peace," <u>New York Times</u> (7 Jan. 1989).

Williams, David. "Japan: Old Ideal, New Reality," <u>Los Angeles Times</u> (11 March 1990).

Wolf, Barbara. "Mishima's Testimony, Wanton and Reverent," <u>The Nation</u> (12 June 1972).